Dear

British
Battleaxes

It takes one to know one!

Christine Hamilton

N R Chamers

The Book of
British
Battleaxes

CHRISTINE HAMILTON

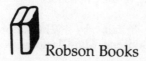

Robson Books

This paperback edition published in 1998 by Robson Books Ltd.

First published in Great Britain in 1997 by Robson Books Ltd,
Bolsover House, 5–6 Clipstone Street, London W1P 8LE

Copyright © 1997 Christine Hamilton

The right of Christine Hamilton to be identified as author of
this work has been asserted by him in accordance with the
Copyright, Designs and Patents Act 1988

British Library Cataloguing in Publication Data
A catalogue record for this title is available from the
British Library

ISBN 1 86105 198 0

Illustrations by John Jensen

Printed in Great Britain by WBC Book
Manufacturers Ltd., Bridgend, Mid-Glamorgan.

Battle Order

Introduction

I do not seek to define the word Battleaxe. Like Humpty Dumpty, when I use a word it means exactly what I want it to mean. For the pedants amongst you, I hasten to add that I am aware the word should be hyphenated but definitely not in the context of this book – you don't interfere with a Battleaxe!

The term Battleaxe was first used around 1910 and it referred then to a very closely defined type: elderly, probably a spinster, aggressive, resentful towards the world, thoroughly unpleasant and pretty ugly to boot!

Cast aside that image! For the purposes of this book, the word Battleaxe covers a multitude of talents, attributes and attitudes. Certain behaviour in a woman attracts attention whereas the same behaviour in a man goes unremarked. Men are supposed to be aggressive and tough, to fight their corner, but any woman who does so is singled out.

I have included some women who, at first glance, may not seem typical Battleaxes. However, for different reasons they, or an episode in their lives, took my fancy, and here they are. They all display the vital attributes; they are tough, determined and self-assured, at least outwardly.

These portraits do not pretend to be scholarly works but they are generally affectionate and approving. As I uncovered the details about each Battleaxe the more I grew to like and admire most of them, each so different in her own way. 'Listen to this,' I would shout. 'She is Maaaaagnificent'.

Some readers, both male and female, will regard some of the

Battleaxes as simply appalling, horrendous, awful and quite beyond the pale. I urge the censorious to suspend judgement and take them all in the spirit in which they are given. The infinite variety of human nature is one of God's greatest gifts and the Battleaxes are an abundant manifestation thereof. Life's rich pattern would be the poorer without them.

As I now appear to be generally regarded as a Battleaxe, I thought it only fair to the others to include a chapter about myself. It would have been unfair of me to write the piece personally so I contracted myself out to a friend who knows me well but upon whom I could rely to be suitably objective. Naturally that person would not dare say anything too horrendous, so, to those who think it is excessively hagiographic, I ask them to be understanding and to bear in mind that its author has to live with a Battleaxe.

The idea for the book came as we drove home to Cheshire up the M40 in late May 1997. My husband, Neil, had been defeated at the I General Election and we were debating what to do with our lives. T had worked as his secrehry for the fourteen years he was in Parliament and I had been at Westminster even longer; a total of 26 years in all.

I started life there when I left university in 1971, as secretary to the late Sir Gerald Nabarro, the flamboyant MP for South Worcestershire. I had spent all my working life in and around the Gothic splendour of the Palace of Westrninster. Suddenly, therefore, after the Election, both Neil and I were unemployed and temporarily floundering in a disconcerting world of job and income insecurity.

The media interest in Neil's election campaign had been intense, indeed worldwide, and it had been a peculiar experience for me to find myself thrust into the glare of the media spotlight for so many weeks. When one is, basically, a kind-hearted, warm, friendly, flirtatious person it is faintly detaching to see oneself portrayed and cartooned as a battling lioness, Lady Muck, a Wife from Hell, akin to Lady Macbeth, a veritable Battleaxe.

Like it or not, it had happened and a personality had been thrust upon me that was far from accurate. However, from that the *Bumper* Book of British Battleaxes was born and, if it gives you pleasure, I am happy to have taken the flak!

There are some notable omissions from the book, for a variety of reasons, and I was very spoilt for choice. The book could have been twice as long and I apologise to anyone who feels I have overlooked a particular favourite. Please let me know – there is always Volume Two.

Christine Hamilton
Nether Alderley

Acknowledgements

Jeremy and Carole Robson, Kate and Charlotte at Robson Books: for their immediate enthusiasm for the project without having seen a word on paper, and for their sustained encouragement and guidance. Without them, this novice would never have completed the course.

Gyles Brandreth: for his encouragement and practical help at a crucial stage.

Peter Carter-Ruck, Andrew Stephenson and Rupert Grey for their unstinting support and loyalty in times of difficulty.

John Jensen: for his inspired cartoons.

Alexandra Erskine, the *Daily Telegraph*'s librarian: for her wonderfully conspiratorial help when the media were bursting to know what I was up to.

My parents: who read the Battleaxes in the early stages, as they were completed one by one, and whose comments and advice were invaluable. Neil had his mother-in-law very much in mind as the book developed.

Finally, a very special word of thanks to my husband, Neil. The challenge of this book enabled me daily to tap into his vast store of peripheral (some might say, useless) knowledge. For several weeks he risked life and limb touching up the Battleaxes. His easy facility with words and his ready wit were always at my disposal. He has been an invaluable inspiration in this, as in all things, and I could never have done it without him.

Dedication

To the thousands of women up and down the country who battle daily against the pressures of life, unknown to the wider world, frequently unappreciated, their virtues unsung. I salute them all.

In particular, to the many forceful women I have known as friends, especially in politics, who display every bit as much courage and determination as those in the book but who are not household names. They know who they are. This book is for them.

Margaret Thatcher

Baroness Thatcher
LG OM FRS

'This woman is headstrong, obstinate and dangerously self-opinionated.'

*****

Margaret Thatcher is the Battleaxe of the Century – perhaps even of the Millennium.

'You've got to put her in the same category as Bloody Mary, Queen Elizabeth I, Queen Anne and Queen Victoria. She reminds me most of Queen Elizabeth I; her handling of men is not dissimilar. I mean, if you had been a courtier of Queen Elizabeth I, you would never have known quite whether you were going to get the treatment of an admired friend or a poke in the eye with an umbrella.' That was Lord Chancellor Hailsham, passing judgement on Margaret Thatcher, having served in her Cabinets from 1979–87.

Others were less flattering. One of her most florid and flatulent critics was Denis Healey, Chancellor of the Exchequer 1974–9, who compared her with Florence Nightingale. 'She stalks through the wards of our hospitals as a lady with a lamp – unfortunately it is a blowlamp.'

In 1983, Healey accused her of the most ambitious piece of social engineering since Stalin and Hitler, claiming she wanted to take us back to the age of Dickens and Victoria, wiping out the social progress made in this century. He declared, 'This is fascism as

Franco established it in Spain. Mrs Thatcher is not just a female Franco but a Pétain in petticoats.' Healey has an avid appetite for abusive, adjectival alliteration as his ardent *aficionados* will appreciate.

Criticising her Foreign Secretary, Sir Geoffrey Howe, for kow-towing to her on Europe in 1984, Healey asked, 'Who is the Mephistopheles behind this shabby Faust?...To quote her own backbenchers, the Great She-Elephant, She-Who-Must-Be-Obeyed, the Catherine the Great of Finchley, the Prime Minister herself.'

Mrs Thatcher was immune to such attacks. She simply brushed them off: 'I always cheer up immensely if an attack is particularly wounding because I think, well, if they attack me personally it means they have not a single argument left.'

When Healey failed to bruise her with the bludgeon of insults, her predecessor as Prime Minister, James Callaghan, tried the rapier of sarcasm. He failed too. When he asked, 'May I congratulate you on being the only man in your team?' she crushed him with the retort: 'Well, that's one more than you've got in yours!'

After she was forced out of office certain leading opponents were prepared to be more magnanimous. Roy Hattersley, Deputy Leader of the Labour Party 1983–92, said with reluctant admiration, 'You could fire a bazooka at her and inflict three large holes. Still she kept coming.'

One leading opponent, however, remains forever intransigent. 'Whatever the lady does is wrong. I do not know of a single right decision taken by her.' Edward Heath deserves a place in the *Guinness Book of Records* for the World's Longest Sulk. For nearly twenty years after she defeated him in the Tory Leadership contest in 1975 he glared at her balefully and bilefully, sitting impassive as an Easter Island stone figure only feet away from her in the House of Commons. He refused to be reconciled.

She was the irresistible force; he was the immovable object. Heath hated her partly because of his personality and partly because she criticised his record. ICI's Personnel Department had rejected Margaret's job application in 1948 on grounds that 'this woman is headstrong, obstinate and dangerously self-opinionated'. That description fits Heath like a sheath (apart from the fact that he is not, of course, a woman). But, a greater source of friction was her rejection of the policies of his Government, in which she had served as Education Secretary from 1970-4.

In 1976, a year after she took Heath's place as Leader of the Opposition, she was asked what she had changed and replied, 'I have changed everything.' Heath was never prepared to admit errors – unlike Margaret Thatcher. After four years in office she readily admitted, 'I'm sure I've made quite a number of mistakes. But I don't think I could just suddenly say what they are now.'

Margaret exulted, 'I am not a consensus politician. I'm a conviction politician.' She despised the Heath Government for its U-turns after 1972, when it sought a corporatist consensus in reaction to the failure of its policy of confronting trade union power. In 1990 she confided, 'It was then that the iron entered my soul.'

In 1978 she said boldly, 'There are still people in my party who believe in consensus politics. I regard them as quislings, as traitors... I mean it.' As Prime Minister she was determined to bulldoze her policies through, come what may. In the deepening recession of 1980, with unemployment at two million and rising, she was urged by the 'wets' to repeat Heath's volte-face of eight years before. She gave them a diamond-hard reply: 'To those waiting with bated breath for that favourite media catchphrase, the U-turn, I have only one thing to say – you turn if you want to; the lady's not for turning.' She underlined her determination by bringing her battle-axe down on the necks of some of the most sodden Cabinet Ministers, showing who was boss once and for all.

She was so unwavering because she had a dream. In this she was endorsed by a surprising source – Tony Benn: 'She believes in something. It is an old-fashioned idea.' She expressed that 'something' very succinctly, 'I came to office with one deliberate intent – to change Britain from a dependent to a self-reliant society, from a "give it to me" to a "do it yourself" nation; to a "get up and go" instead of a "sit back and wait" Britain.' She saw herself as a kind of bracing cold bath into which the nation should be plunged. Only a woman of the most exceptional drive could have carried on charging ahead against the almost united opposition of the defeatist British Establishment.

Her strength was satirised in TV programmes like *Spitting Image*. One episode portrayed her at a restaurant table with the rest of the Cabinet gibbering around her. The waiter came to take her order. She roared, 'Raw steak with plenty of blood.' He then asked, 'What about the vegetables, Madam?' Looking at the Cabinet, she replied, with a dismissive wave of the hand, 'They'll have the same.'

This lampooning was water off a duck's back to her. She knew what she had to do and just got on with it, saying, 'I think sometimes the Prime Minister should be intimidating. There's not much point being a weak, floppy thing in the chair, is there?' Lord Carrington was asked in the early 1980s what would happen if Mrs Thatcher was run down by a bus. He correctly replied, 'No bus would dare!' Former US Secretary of State, George Schultz, confided, 'If I were married to her I'd be sure and have the dinner on the table when she came home.'

Margaret Thatcher explained her *Führerprinzip*, 'You cannot have my job and have had a vision, a dream, a will to turn Britain around, to live up to the best of herself, without being more than a chairman of a committee . . . a Prime Minister has a task of leadership. If the trumpet gives an uncertain sound who shall prepare himself to the battle? . . . If one has a sense of purpose, they call that authoritarianism. It is totally false, but there you are . . . Success is not an attractive thing to many people.'

'And, of course, some of them are snobs. They can never forgive me for coming from a very ordinary background. It does not bother me at all. I cannot stand snobbery of any kind.' When she sacked Christopher Soames in 1981 she 'got the distinct impression that he felt the natural order of things was being violated and he was being dismissed by his housemaid'.

Much of the academic establishment felt similarly disdainful about her and, in spite of her being one of the most distinguished alumni of Oxford University, a spiteful campaign was successfully organised to deny her a proposed Honorary Degree. This did not discomfit her one bit. As she told the Conservative Party Conference, 'I went to Oxford University, but I've never let that hold me back.'

Her robustness was particularly evident in her dealings with foreigners when defending British interests. She drove European leaders to distraction by her relentless hectoring. But she usually got her way. In Dublin in 1980 she harangued them for four whole hours at a working dinner, and then again through three full meetings of the Council of Ministers over two days to get a refund on Britain's contribution to the European Budget. Margaret summed up another Dublin Summit ten years later, 'You get a long way by nagging – nobody argued with me.'

Denis Healey poked fun at her, 'The Prime Minister says that she has given the French President a piece of her mind – this is not a gift I would receive with alacrity.' But more often than not it worked. President Mitterrand observed, 'She has the eyes of Caligula and the mouth of Marilyn Monroe.' Mrs Thatcher was perhaps aware of the effect of the eyes. She had the swivel chairs in the London QEII Conference Centre removed and replaced with light wooden ones because she 'always thought there was something to be said for looking at your opposite number in the eye without his being able to swivel sideways to escape'.

Her relish for confronting the foreigner did not, however, preclude a sense of humour. Kenneth Clarke lamented Britain's defeat by Germany in the 1990 World Cup football semi-finals, 'Isn't it terrible being beaten by the Germans at our national sport, Prime Minister?' Margaret consoled him by saying, 'I shouldn't worry about it too much, dear. We've beaten them twice this century at theirs.'

The defining moment of the Thatcher years was the Falklands War in 1982. The Russians had dubbed her 'the Iron Lady' long before she became Prime Minister and she relished the title. But despite her fearsome reputation, decades of national defeatism made many people doubt that she would have either the will to send a Naval Task Force 8000 miles to the South Atlantic, or the stamina to fight the war to a successful conclusion.

When the crisis broke, Enoch Powell declared dramatically in the House of Commons, 'The Prime Minister, shortly after she came into office, received a soubriquet as the "Iron Lady". It arose in the context of remarks which she made about defence against the Soviet Union and its allies; but there was no reason to suppose that she did not welcome and, indeed, take pride in the description. In the next week or two this House, the nation and she herself will learn of what metal she is made.'

After the war had been won he rose again: 'Is the Prime Minister aware that the report has now been received from the public analyst on a certain substance recently subjected to analysis and that I have obtained a copy of the report? It shows that the substance under test consisted of ferrous metal of the highest quality. It is of exceptional tensile strength, resistant to wear-and-tear and to stress, and may be used to advantage for all national purposes.'

His opinion was shared by the military professionals. The Chief of the Defence Staff, Admiral of the Fleet Lord Lewin said, 'She was a decisive leader, which of course is what the military want. We don't want a wishy-washy decision, we want a clear-cut decision and we want it quickly. She was magnificent in her support of the military.'

At home Margaret Thatcher displayed equal intransigence in dealing with Arthur Scargill's attempt to overthrow the government by a revolutionary coal strike. 'In the Falklands we had to fight the enemy without. Here the enemy is within and it is much more difficult to fight, but just as dangerous to liberty.' 'What we've got is an attempt to substitute the rule of the mob for the rule of the law. It must not succeed.' It did not. By meticulous preparation and determination to fight to the finish she destroyed Scargill and his strike.

The Liberal leader, David Steel, thought her single-mindedness a defect: 'Trying to tell the Prime Minister anything is like making an important phone-call and getting an answering machine.' Margaret would no doubt respond that, if you have strongly defined beliefs, you fight for them all the way and compromise, if at all, only as a last resort. She said (and it may not have been a joke), 'I am extraordinarily patient – provided that I get my own way in the end.'

Another defining moment occurred when she was nearly assassinated by an IRA bomb at the 1984 Conservative Party Conference in Brighton. She emerged from her half-demolished hotel, perfectly composed, coiffed and dressed, to declare, 'Now it must be business as usual.' The conference continued; she made her speech as planned and her hostility to the IRA remained resolute and implacable.

Such tales may give the impression of an unfeeling woman. Nothing could be further from the truth as many who have had personal contact with her will testify. She cares and is very conscious of the negative interpretation of her strengths. She once told an interviewer 'Please don't use the word "tough". People might get the impression that I don't care. And I do care very deeply. "Resilient" I think.'

During the 1992 General Election campaign, Margaret went walkabout in Stockport, where she had been attacked by a protester, who had hit her on the head with a bunch of daffodils. The police went into overdrive, as it could so easily have been a weapon. Margaret was completely unfazed. As she said, 'It was so hard on the daffodils.'

By 1990, after eleven exhilarating years of taking the nation by the scruff of the neck, she was unceremoniously turfed out. John Biffen said, 'She was a tigress surrounded by hamsters'. The agent of her downfall was Sir Geoffrey Howe, whose previous attacks Denis Healey likened to 'being savaged by a dead sheep'. For the first time in history a tigress was savaged to death by an alliance of 167 hamsters and one dead sheep. (In the leadership ballot in 1990 204 MPs voted for Margaret, 152 for Michael Heseltine and 16 abstained). Cecil Parkinson analysed why she was forced out: 'The Labour Party is led by a pygmy and we are led by a giant. We have decided that the answer to our problems is to find a pygmy of our own.'

She was fatally undermined by those who worked closest with her, namely much of the Cabinet. They were likened to Nasser's chief of staff who said his position was 100 per cent loyalty – until the time for treachery arrives.

Her daughter, Carol's, opinion struck a chord with many: 'After all she's done, I think this is an act of gutless treachery. As far as I'm concerned Tory is now a four letter word.' A Thatcher loyalist's letter in *The Times* was to the point: 'The gentlemen in grey suits should now be visited by gentlemen in white coats.' Ann

Widdecombe identified the difference between the Prime Battleaxe and her windy backbenchers: 'I think the rest of the world will think we are mad and indeed we are. We've turned out the greatest Prime Minister in the post-war years simply because of short-term nerves.'

Although treachery nestles in every Cabinet or Court, in her early years she had been able to rely totally on Willie Whitelaw as Deputy Prime Minister. She had defeated him to become Leader and he represented the old landed, patrician interest which Margaret's revolution engulfed. Despite that, Whitelaw was unflinchingly loyal to her ever after. At a valedictory dinner on Whitelaw's retirement in 1991 Margaret caused riotous mirth by enthusing, 'Every Prime Minister needs a Willie.' She enjoyed the joke as much as the rest of the company – when it was explained to her!

Although he was desperate for her to win because that was what she wanted, her ever-faithful husband, Denis, was glad to have his wife back. He had always provided a leavening of interests outside politics. A sharp and successful businessman, he was able to provide in private a fund of shrewd advice and penetrating comment.

The 'Dear Bill' caricature was well wide of the mark but gave rise to some good stories, to which Denis sometimes played up, about golf and the 'nineteenth hole'. A Tory Party worker, winning no prizes for tact, once asked him, 'Mr Thatcher, I understand you have a drink problem.' Denis's robust response was, 'Yes, madam, I have. There is never enough of it.' Another asked him how he spent his time. 'Well, when I'm not completely pissed I like to play a lot of golf.' He turned the *Private Eye* caricature of him as a buffoon to good advantage, as it enabled him to give advice without falling into the Hillary Clinton trap of appearing to be a power behind the throne.

Margaret found it difficult at first to cope with working less than an 18 hour day. She had always been a workaholic. In 1983 the Queen had said to Cecil Parkinson, 'They tell me you have influence with the Prime Minister. She must take a proper holiday and if you will speak to her about it so will I.'

After four years out of office she still had itchy fingers. In

February 1995 she announced, 'I've just had the honour of delivering the speech at Ronald Reagan's 84th birthday celebrations. I'm only 69, just the age Ronald was when he became President and I must say I'm feeling a little underemployed.'

Ronald Reagan and Margaret Thatcher danced through the political minefields of the 1980s like Fred Astaire and Ginger Rogers. They were perfectly in step with one another. The Iron Lady enthusiastically backed Reagan's identification of the Soviet Union as an Evil Empire. As a Warrior Queen she firmly supported his massive build-up of technological weaponry and the deployment of nuclear missiles in Europe. The Soviet Union could not compete and collapsed, thus ending the Cold War.

Thatcher had an enormous influence on Reagan and not just because they were soul-mates. He also feared the lash of her tongue. Even the threat of an ear-bashing on the telephone could influence him. Frank Carlucci, US Defence Secretary, reminded him during the Irangate scandal that, if he took a particular course of action, Mrs Thatcher would be on the phone immediately. 'Oh, I don't want that!' was his petrified response.

Prime Ministers lead necessarily cocooned lives. When normal life resumes the transition is often perplexing. Margaret was, of course, more than equal to the problems. Carol once asked her: 'Can you manage the supermarket shopping, Mum?' and got the reply, 'Good heavens, yes, dear, I've opened enough of them.' As she told Eve Pollard in 1991, 'One is an ordinary person – and don't you forget it.'

'Ordinary' is the one thing Margaret Thatcher is not. Few individuals give their name to an 'ism.' She altered the political landscape not only in Britain but throughout the world. Not least, she had a profound effect on the British Labour Party. As she wryly observed of them in December 1996, 'I am so pleased that after four election defeats they have now come to terms with the 1980s. Perhaps after four more they will come to terms with the 1990s. I am told we are all Thatcherites now. My goodness me, never has the road to Damascus been so congested.'

One of her closest acolytes, Nicholas Ridley, lamented her political passing: 'The nation was oppressed by many dragons in

1979. Margaret Thatcher came forth to slay them. After she had slain them the nation no longer had need of her. Normal humdrum government has been resumed. We shall miss her style of government.'

But perhaps the most eloquent testimonial she received was from Geoffrey Howe (speaking three years before he wielded the assassin's knife): 'History will surely recognise her achievements as Britain's first woman Prime Minister, a leader with the courage of her convictions, who assailed the conventional wisdom of her day, challenged and overthrew the existing order, changed the political map, and put her country on its feet again.'

She battled, and won, against ignorance and prejudice; against communism, dictatorship and socialism; against vested interests and union bullying; against Euro-nonsense and the nanny state; against General Galtieri and Saddam Hussein. As she said herself in 1979: 'If someone is confronting our essential liberties, if someone is inflicting injuries and harm, by God I'll confront them.'

She is the Supreme Battleaxe.

Dame Barbara Cartland

*'Look. I am a Star. People expect me to dress like one, and that's it. I
cannot go out looking like an ordinary member of the public.'*

*****

Dame Barbara is not just a star, she is a super-nova – a stellar
explosion which can eclipse in brightness all its surroundings. She
is truly spectacular, with her make-up apparently applied with a
palette-knife, her vermilion lips and positively vast false spidery
eyelashes ('like two crows crashing into the white cliffs of Dover').
She is show-stopping as no other woman can ever hope to be,
caparisoned in voluminous swathes of vivid fuchsia pink and
clouds of bright turquoise chiffon, studded with glittering *diamanté*
and piled high with costume jewellery (she sold the real stuff). She
is a modern equivalent of one of the seven wonders of the ancient
world – the hanging gardens of Babylon perhaps.

Her addiction to bright pinks and scarab blue followed a visit to
Tutankhamun's tomb in 1927, where she beheld the wonders of the
late Pharaoh's taste in colour. Colour affects the character and
personality of the person and, in tribute to Dame Barbara, an entire
prison in Colorado has been painted pink because it has such a
beneficial effect on the inmates.

Born in the last year of Queen Victoria's reign, she became a
débutante in 1919, her father having been killed in the war the
previous year. Her mother had very little money and they rented a
tall gloomy house in Kensington for four guineas a week. The

young Barbara did not let that interfere with her instinctive gaiety and sense of fun. She danced at the Savoy, the Berkeley and the Café de Paris. She dined at Quaglino's, where she found a pearl in her oyster, and the Prince of Wales with his mistress.

The family were grand but virtually penniless and, at the sensible suggestion of her mother that she should earn some money, the star of the romantic novel was born. Her first, published in 1923, went into six editions and five languages. After that she began to write seriously and to make money even more seriously.

She attracted and collected celebrities after finding favour with Lord Beaverbrook (she wrote gossip for the *Daily Express*), dining with him and his cronies from the 1920s.

She was first presented at Court in 1925, in a dress given to her by the young Norman Hartnell who had recently opened a shop in Bruton Street. Presentation was essential. Un-presented gels were simply not acceptable at British Embassies throughout the world and they could not be asked to Buckingham Palace Garden Parties.

In 1930 she designed and produced the first Pageant since the war, in aid of the British Legion. Most of the great industries were represented and Barbara persuaded society beauties to wear her designs. In her own words: 'The Marchioness Curzon of Kedlestone was Wool. Lady Ashley represented Coal. The Countess of Bective was Machinery. Paper looked lovely on Viscountess Castlerosse. I wore an enormous steamship of the White Star Line.'

Earlier, when 23, she married Alexander McCorquodale. It was her fiftieth proposal but, as she correctly observed,: 'You can't marry everybody can you?' She divorced him in 1933 and subsequently married his cousin, Hugh (her fifty-sixth proposal).

Divorce was a high risk venture in those days and could have dashed her hopes both socially and financially. But it was imperative. Alexander was a disappointment to her. 'Men are at their best in the middle of the day . . . but he was a secret drinker, so he wasn't a lover. He was very sweet to me but he didn't go to bed. Well, once in a blue moon.' The blue moon did luminesce once and they produced a daughter, Raine ('How tiresome, all mothers prefer sons'). Her second marriage to Hugh lasted for twenty-eight perfect years, – 'due to my special vitamins and honey' – and produced two cherished sons.

Her daughter, Raine, married well in 1948. Owing to the complexities of the British peerage, without changing her husband, she changed her name thrice, becoming successively the Hon. Mrs Legge, the Viscountess Lewisham and the Countess of Dartmouth. Raine subsequently married Earl Spencer, father of Diana, Princess of Wales. Dame Barbara vigorously defends her daughter against the charge of social climbing. 'What nonsense. After all, she exchanged a ninth Earl for an eighth.'

Asked for her comments on Raine's third husband, the Comte de Chambrun, she opined: 'All Frenchmen are charming. Some are more charming than others. Some have money and some don't. He doesn't.' Predictably (perhaps due to an absence of vitamins and honey) Raine's third marriage, in 1993, did not last.

However, when a friend expressed sorrow at the divorce of her son Ian from his wife of many years she snapped, 'Don't be sorry for her. She came with nothing and left with millions.'

Despite her worship of romance, Dame Barbara is a ruthlessly unsentimental observer, with a keen eye and a caustic wit. A genius for publicity, she is also brilliant at caricature and unafraid to turn this on herself. She is one of the last great female eccentrics in the land.

As well as her prodigious output of novels, she answers 40,000 letters a year. 'I have four secretaries. They are all women and all hopeless. I would love to employ a man but how could they take dictation from me in the bath?'

She is the perfect chauvinist and her love of the opposite sex transcends intellectual matters. As she races towards her 'century not out' she would still rather have lunch with a stupid man than a clever woman.

An advocate of 'alternative medicine' long before it was fashionable, she takes 60 vitamin pills a day and says she has 'the body of a young girl. I ought to be photographed naked but I think that would be too much for the press.' She attributes this as much to her miracle cream, Ayesha's Flame – dedicated to the Goddess of Eternal Youth – as to the pills.

Concerned to learn that 'those idiot doctors have given her a general anaesthetic', she sent the Queen Mother a consignment of brain pills (Celaton CH3 TRI-Plus) when she left hospital in 1993 after an operation to remove a fish bone from her throat. 'I have been taking three a day for years. They stop one going gaga.'

She was appalled at malnutrition during the war and has been an evangelist ever since for the cause of dietary supplements.

'Vegetarians, of course, are a perfect damn nuisance. In Europe, the tallest and strongest men are the Germans and they eat a lot of meat.'

On the political front, Dame Barbara takes full credit for bringing back prayers into state schools in 1989. 'I was supported in this only by the *Daily Star*. No bishop or clergyman had anything to say on the subject.' She alerted all MPs, receiving 400 replies to her letter and, as a direct result, the Lords and Commons voted to reinstate prayers into state school assemblies.

In 1995 she demanded, in a letter in the *Daily Telegraph*, that the Archbishop of York should resign as he was 'trying to upset the prayers I brought back into the state schools'. It seems to me, she wrote, 'that the sooner he resigns from the Church of England and we have priests who believe, as they always did in the old days, that God is there to help us, the better.'

She takes some credit for the Tories' election victory in 1992, when she rumbled Neil Kinnock's atheism and denounced him in the columns of virtually every local paper up and down the land. 'I decidedly increased the Conservative vote.'

Despite what she regarded as a momentary lapse of manners on his part (he had addressed her in a letter as 'Dear Barbara' when they had met but once) she invited John Major to luncheon at her Hertfordshire home, Camfield Place. For the Dame this was no mere social occasion; she had business to transact – the moral salvation of the nation. It was at this lunch that the Prime Minister's ill-fated Back to Basics campaign was born.

If only he had put her in charge how different things might have been. Instead, he messed it up by ignoring her advice that it should be called Back to Romance. 'Basics' has quite the wrong connotation and this was absolutely the one thing Dame Barbara wanted to avoid. 'Never in our whole history have things been as bad as they are at the moment. That's because people will talk about sex, sex, sex all the time and not about love. Good old-fashioned morality is what we want. Good manners, men opening doors for women, love, love, love.'

She abhors the idea of a classless society but reluctantly accepts that things have changed. 'Class? Class? Of course there will always be class. But we now have a society of opportunity. Otherwise, how do you suppose a common little man like John King gets to be Chairman of British Airways?'

She gave short shrift to an interviewer who ventured to ask whether she thought class barriers had broken down. 'Of course they have. If they hadn't someone like you wouldn't be interviewing someone like me.'

She was appalled when the Royal Opera House decided to throw open the Royal Box, when not being used for the intended purpose, to the paying classes. 'I think it is just cheap and shoddy and should be stopped immediately.'

Her excitement at 'joining' the Royal Family when her step-granddaughter married the Prince of Wales soon dissipated as the marriage crumbled. In 1994 she wrote an impassioned letter to much of the nation's press imploring the Prince and Princess of Wales to stay together and put the good of their country and their children before personal feelings. Amazingly, despite ending her letter with 'God Save England and The Queen', she was ignored.

She even wrote an open letter to her step-granddaughter, via the columns of *Hello!*, beseeching her to think of England and the future of the Royal Family. 'If we lose the Royal Family...we shall just be an unimportant little island with a flag.'

She lays some of the blame for the breakdown of the marriage on the fact that the Prince of Wales was 'sent to that ghastly school where he never met any of his own class. Had he gone to Eton instead of Gordonstoun he would have met lots of dukes and, more importantly, their sisters.' She appears, with this remark, to have overlooked the fact that Lady Diana was the daughter of an earl.

More recently she was comforted when, commenting on the millions raised by the sale of the Princess of Wales' dresses at Christie's, her son Ian reassured her, 'But Mummy, your eyelashes will fetch twice as much.'

She wrote in one of her novels 'Although a man may seek the purity of the lily he would be inhuman if he refused the other flowers he encountered by the roadside.' Roughly translated for the modern world, she declares that 'A Man should not be a virgin on his wedding night. You want one person who knows what he is doing.'

She has, to date, written about 680 books, including five autobiographies but as she is only 97 there will undoubtedly be many more. For her, writing books is very easy. 'When I have finished one book I simply ask God to send me a plot for the next one, and it's there.'

She has over 750 million sales worldwide and shows absolutely no sign of reducing her prodigious output. Although her books are read less in Britain than formerly, that decline is more than compensated for by soaring sales abroad, in places like China where 'they are less interested in sex, sex, sex – at least the Government censors are and that is what matters'. This policy may not be good for long-term sales because, without the sex there will be no readers.

She has long been in the *Guinness Book of Records* as the top selling author worldwide and the most prolific – breaking the world record for the last 17 years by writing an average of 23 books a year. She has the longest entry in *Who's Who*, consuming an entire page.

She reigns supreme over the world of romance from her sumptuous home, Camfield Place, built in 1867 on the site of a Tudor manor house. This was the home of Beatrix Potter's grandfather, so Dame Barbara is the proud custodian of Mr McGregor's garden, surrounded by its high Tudor brick walls and containing the hole in the fence through which Peter Rabbit used to squeeze.

She has put her formidable talents to good use over the years. She has been a County Councillor and a wartime welfare offlcer; she campaigned for gypsy chiidren to have proper education; invented the idea and administered a pool of white wedding dresses for Service brides during the war; she worked with the St John Ambulance Brigade for decades. She even carried the first glider mail in her aeroplane-towed glider, named 'Barbara Cartland' from Manston Aerodrome to Reading in June 1931.

Barbara Cartland acquired the official accolade of Battleaxedom in 1991, when she was made a Dame Commander of the Most Excellent Order of the British Empire for 'her contribution to literature and her work for humanitarian and charitable causes'. Practical as ever, she said, 'It should have happened years ago. What's the point of giving it to you when you're nearly dead.'

Imperious, opinionated, indefatigable, unstoppable, unique – of course! Nearly dead? Never! She must be immortal.

Nicola Foulston

*'It is almost impossible for anyone to make me feel intimidated. I am
brilliant in a war cabinet. Good in a war zone. Great with
confrontation.'*

*****

This 'feisty little monster' became, aged only 29, the youngest ever
Winner of the Veuve Cliquot Businesswoman of the Year Award in
1997.

Direct, determined and self-reliant, Nicola grew up in Surrey. Her
father, John Foulston, had experienced some difficult times in
various businesses. One day the family had furniture and the next
orange boxes. But, when Nicola was about nine, his computer
leasing business, Atlantic Computers, took off and the family
fortunes began rising rapidly. He eventually amassed a £40m
fortune by selling it on.

Nicola went to the Royal Naval School at Haslemere. She had
failed Common Entrance because of her maths. Despite that
setback, her parents managed to secure her a place – which was
retrospectively justified when she went on to read Maths at London
University. However, the academic ivory tower did not appeal and
'sheer boredom' set in.

She wanted to work and dropped out to help her father, who
gave her charge of a company which restored old racing cars. It was
losing about £300,000 a year when she took over at the age of 18 but,
by the end of her first year in control, it was breaking even.

John Foulston's passion was motor racing. He spent part of his new fortune buying Brands Hatch for £5m in 1986. Tragically, a year later he was killed in a crash at Silverstone whilst driving a classic racing car, a single-seater open-topped McLaren. Nicola was just 19, the eldest of three children.

Like her father, she was strong, dominant and aggressive, all characteristics on which she capitalised. 'It is almost impossible for anyone to make me feel intimidated. I am brilliant in a war cabinet. Good in a war zone. Great with confrontation.'

Her father's death hurt her terribly but she was determined not to allow his enthusiasm to perish with him. She battled it out with her mother to be allowed to join the Brands Hatch Board and, once the MD departed, Nicola was in total control at the tender age of 20 She bought her mother out. She shook up the 'blazer-and-cravat' brigade of the male motor-racing establishment, shocking them rigid with her view that sport should take second place to business and profit.

She was 'headstrong, tenacious and brimming with ambition'. Looking back she says, 'I was young and arrogant. I could do anything.' Youth was a disadvantage so she wore glasses to make herself look older.

A 'bold booming character, usually dressed in vividly colourful clothes', Nicola aims to turn Brands Hatch into another Alton Towers, a serious money-making machine with hands-on reality experiences – 'someone else working the controls is old hat'. Not surprisingly she was greeted with hostility from the men, the die-hard enthusiasts who see motor sport as more of a religion than an entertainment.

She resents the degree of influence exerted by amateurs. She would like to convert the 350 volunteer marshals into employees – because she could then sack them if they are rude to the customers! 'An accident on the track is their moment of glory. It can take half an hour to do a five-minute job and it's the spectators who suffer. I now fine clubs if they still have wreckage on the circuit that's disrupting the racing after ten minutes.'

Her mission was to complete her father's work and see Brands Hatch floated on the Stock Exchange. 'It was all pretty horrendous when I took over, a complete mess. It was crisis after crisis . . . firefighting.' She now regrets not being even tougher when she started. 'I had a choice. Either to get rid of all the bad people by firing them all at once, or to do it over time. I did it over time which was wrong because we sustained the problem for longer.'

Under her direction the company has prospered and now makes around £2m profit a year. A new HQ and conference centre have been built, the race track modernised, tables turned on the TV contracts so they now pay her (not vice versa), and exhibitions and corporate hospitality abound. Brands Hatch went public in autumn 1996, realising her father's dream.

She was enraged by fans who arrived at each race meeting with their own refreshments, not giving a penny to the in-house caterers. She invented the Hatchburger to tantalise their tastebuds and the money came in.

Foulston says she encountered more ageism than sexism. 'I am not aware of any prejudice or that people are patronising to me because I am a woman.' Whether they were or were not, she wisely ignored it and pressed on to success.

'Nicola is a feisty woman. She has a remarkable ability to walk into a room of suits, all pumping testosterone, and make them too terrified to disagree with her.'

'I make decisions fast. Sometimes I make ten decisions and only get eight right. I'm a strong leader. I don't faff around.'

She could not be a supermodel but is needlessly self-deprecating about her figure. 'I'm not a worrier. Nervous people are always thin because they don't eat.' She claims to have a short attention span – if someone is trying to get their point across she gives them about four seconds.

She partly attributes her strength to having been bullied at school as she coped with the transition from State to private education. She was beaten around the head with hockey sticks, which she found a character-building experience.

With an image that owes more to *Dynasty* than Damon Hill, Nicola could teach Sue Ellen a thing or two about power-dressing. She enjoys clothes but, as with her men, she makes them work for her. 'I am a loud person with a reputation for wearing strong colours. Her clothes shout 'Don't push me. I mean business'. She dresses to demonstrate she is the boss, she is in control. One person who can stand up to her is her housekeeper who has apparently banned her from shopping because 'she has so many clothes'. She now claims to hate shopping, except for books which she rarely has time to read.

'Bubbly, talkative and flirtatious,' she admits to getting on much better with men than women. Personal happiness in marriage has eluded her so far. A woman in a hurry, she took flying lessons, aiming to cut down the travelling time between racing circuits. In the process she fell in love with and married her instructor, Craig Sergeant. They crash-landed in divorce within 18 months. She takes responsibility for the breakdown, blaming her high octane 70 hour working week lifestyle. 'I wasn't very good at compromising. I am too selfish.'

She currently declares she has been immunised against marriage but might have children in due course in a stable relationship; but not until she is prepared to lay down some of the reins of business and spend time with them.

She admires women who combine work and family but holds traditional views on the roles of a husband and wife within a marriage. She does not believe she can combine a fulfilling family life with the demands of her career. 'It would not be fair on me or on any children.' She does not presume to tell others what to do, but has predictably been lambasted by feminists for suggesting that mothers should give up work and stay at home to look after their children.

Although insisting she is as tough as ever, she has recognised a certain mellowing. She happily admits she had 'a hell of a temper' and could act childishly. She admits being 'not very good at interpersonal skills. I'm very bad at saying "Well done." But I'm lucky. I have a team of people who believe in me even though I may upset them on a daily basis.' She never bears grudges.

She sleeps in the nude and is quick to dismiss the glamour of racing drivers. 'You should stand by the car when the drivers get out. Believe me, there is nothing more unattractive than this sweaty tired, red-faced creature. I know, I've had to present the garlands and kiss the sweaty faces.'

The Empress Matilda
(b. 1102 – d.1167)

'She was a termagant – haughty, tactless, grasping and insolent.'
*****

Matilda cut a swathe through twelfth century England, using real battle-axes to seize the throne on the death of her father, King Henry I. Sadly, there were neither editors nor tabloid newspapers in those days, as the family life of the Plantagenets was vastly more diverting than that of the Windsors.

Matilda's grandfather was William the Bastard, who changed his name to 'William the Conqueror' in 1066, in a bid to gain medieval middle-class respectability. On William's death, his eldest son, Robert, was considered too good-natured, easy-going and prone to take the line of least resistance to become king of England. So he was pushed aside in favour of his younger brother, William Rufus.

Rufus had what it took to be a successful monarch – he was cynical, vain, capricious and ill-tempered, with no taste for activities other than hunting and military exercises. In an Age of Faith he was a blasphemer who scoffed at religion. The chronicler, William of Malmesbury, recorded that the King surrounded himself with young chums who 'rivalled women in delicacy of person, minced their gait, walked with loose gesture and half-naked'. They also wore long hair and invented the fashion of shoes with curved points.

William of Malmesbury was the twelfth-century equivalent of Kelvin of Fleet Street. Unfortunately he lacked the pithy genius of a *Sun* headline writer. As an investigative illuminated-parchment-scribe on the 'Newes of the Olde Worlde' he should have had a field-day with lurid stories about the 'troops of pathics (rent-boys) and droves of harlots who followed the court.' Alas! there were no paparazzi with telephoto lenses to record the goings-on at what the *Sun* would undoubtedly have called 'Poofter Bill's Pansy Palace'.

Rufus met a violent death – killed (probably murdered) by an arrow whilst hunting in the New Forest. He was lucky not to suffer the end of other medieval homosexuals like his descendant Edward II, who was put to death in the customary way – a red-hot poker up the backside.

He was succeeded by Henry I, his younger brother and Matilda's father, who had probably planned Rufus' murder. Henry I was a good king – but grasping, cruel and lascivious. For a time he was persuaded to give up his mistresses and lead a respectable life with his queen (also, just to confuse things, called Matilda). But the joys of monogamy soon palled. By the time of his death in 1135 Henry had fathered at least 21 children, but only two were legitimate – a son who perished at sea in 1120 and Matilda, who survived him.

There was little relish in England for a female ruler, especially as Matilda was virtually a stranger, having left the country at the age of eight to be brought up in Germany, being betrothed to the future Holy Roman Emperor. She was a termagant – haughty, tactless, grasping and insolent. Henry I nevertheless forced his barons to swear to recognise his daughter as their Queen upon his death.

Her first husband, Emperor Henry V, died in 1125. At his death he placed his sceptre in her hands, seemingly to indicate that he wished her to succeed him. The German princes thrilled to the prospect of a dominatrix to discipline them. But her father had other ideas for his only legitimate child, now a widow, and called her back to England. He wished to neutralise Anjou, long a troublesome neighbour of Normandy, by marrying her off to Geoffrey, the son and heir of its Count.

Matilda's first husband (the Emperor) had been 30 years older than her; her second, Geoffrey, was 11 years younger, a high-spirited lad of 14, who did not relish marriage to this disagreeable and haughty woman of 25. He found life with her intolerable and, after two years, sent her packing. In due course, for political reasons, Geoffrey asked her to return. Henry I (her father), despairing of finding another husband for her, decided to consent. Henry of Huntingdon (another chronicler) says that 'she was given a reception fitting for such a virago'.

Geoffrey and Matilda lived in enough amity to produce three children in quick succession, including the future Henry II of England. Henry I was overjoyed that the succession now seemed assured. But Matilda contrived to poison the happiness of his last two years by stirring up trouble between her father and her husband. She first demanded that Henry hand over various castles and then virtually the whole of the Duchy of Normandy as her infant son's birthright.

In the autumn of 1135 she had a violent quarrel with her father and stormed off in a fury to Anjou. They were never reconciled as he died from a surfeit of lampreys on 1 December. Matilda immediately entered Normandy to claim her inheritance. Matilda's second marriage had been unpopular in England and her subsequent behaviour incensed the barons. They could not face her as Queen and opted instead for her cousin, Stephen of Blois, who had set out for England immediately on hearing of Henry's death. He was crowned just before Christmas 1135.

Matilda appealed unsuccessfully to the Pope for recognition as the rightful Queen. Following his rebuff she devoted herself diligently to stirring up trouble for Stephen. By 1138 many barons had already deserted him on account of his weakness and transferred their allegiance to her. In September 1139 she landed at Arundel with 140 knights to contest the throne, conveniently putting up with her stepmother who had a castle there. Stephen first besieged her but then foolishly allowed her free passage to join her brother at Bristol. She repaid him by immediately beginning a war of plundering raids, burning of towns and besieging of castles.

At the battle of Lincoln in 1141, Stephen idiotically threw away the advantage arising from his occupation of high ground and he descended to the marshy plain for a 'fair fight'. (Like Sir Austen

Chamberlain, 'he always played the game and always lost'.) He was disastrously defeated and was dragged before Matilda, who did not repay him with the magnanimity he had shown to her. She sent him in chains into captivity in Bristol castle. This was a decisive development and she controlled the country for about a year afterwards. But, her behaviour was so arrogant and high-handed that she alienated all those whose support she might have gained and needed to confirm her conquest.

She confiscated lands and honours ruthlessly; she offended the barons who came to pay homage to her with the haughty coldness of her demeanour; she turned a deaf ear to the pleas of Stephen's wife and his brother for mercy towards him and his children; she rejected with withering scorn a reasonable request from the citizens of London for a renewal of 'King Edward the Confessor's Laws', demanded from them a heavy subsidy and, when they protested, drove them from her presence with a torrent of abuse. As a result they rose in revolt and drove her from the city.

She set off for Winchester, to subdue its Bishop who had changed sides back to Stephen, but she was besieged so effectively whilst there that her troops were driven to the verge of starvation. They cut their way out of the city, sustaining heavy losses, and Matilda escaped to Gloucester. She was half dead with fatigue and, to throw her pursuers off the scent, was carried into the city on a bier, tied with ropes as though she were a corpse.

The following winter she escaped to Oxford, where she was later besieged again by Stephen in September 1142. By Christmas, with deep snow on the ground, the garrison was on the verge of starvation. Matilda escaped this time by dropping down over the castle wall disguised in a white sheet and audaciously made her way unrecognised across the frozen Thames and through the heart of Stephen's camp.

In her few months of power whilst Stephen had been imprisoned, she irretrievably damaged her own cause by her outrageous conduct. Anarchy gripped England because of Stephen's weakness and vacillation and a series of revolts by great magnates unleashed an orgy of destruction and terror over vast tracts of the country. Circumstances ought to have been propitious as the country yearned for order, this being supposedly a time 'when Christ and his saints were asleep'. Nevertheless, Matilda was still able to generate no enthusiasm for her cause. She lingered in England another five years and then retired to Normandy in 1148.

Arnulf of Lisieux wrote that she was 'a woman who had nothing of the woman in her'. Her personal courage and steely nerve were displayed on more than one occasion. On the other hand, her arrogant and tactless treatment of her cousin, Henri of Blois, Bishop of Winchester, a prince of the Church and a fellow descendant of the Conqueror, displayed an impenetrable stupidity which probably cost her the crown. She similarly offended her uncle David (King of Scots) and her brother, the Earl of Gloucester and many lesser mortals.

After her son Henry II assumed the dukedom of Normandy in 1150 and then the throne of England in 1154, Matilda's harsh and violent temper mellowed and she developed a real nobility of character, culminating in the taking of the veil. However badly she had advised herself when seeking to become Queen of England, she gave her son good advice – not least in warning him against appointing Thomas Becket Archbishop of Canterbury.

Matthew Parris (the medieval one) recorded her significance in her epitaph: 'Here lies Henry's daughter, wife, mother; great by birth, greater by marriage, greatest by motherhood.' Although but dimly known today, she is one of the greatest Battleaxes of English history.

Ann Widdecombe

'I am overweight. I am ugly. I am dumpy. I have crooked teeth. I am 49. I am a spinster. But what the hell.'

*****

At barely five feet one inch tall, Ann Widdecombe is, by her own unflattering description, a Pocket Battleaxe. She has been branded a monster for her uncompromising hard-line views. The *Daily Mirror* even went so far as to nickname her Doris Karloff, after the legendary Frankenstein film-star Boris. The *Daily Mail* described her as 'resembling an Albanian goalie'.

Even in an admiring portrait she does not escape – Petronella Wyatt said that she was 'terrifically mobile, like a Womble on speed' or 'like an unpopular Latin mistress out of Angela Brazil'.

One person with whom she is probably unpopular is former Home Secretary, Michael Howard MP. With one devastating lunge she single-handedly killed stone dead his bid for the Tory leadership after the 1997 General Election.

Until 1 May she was one of Howard's deputies as Minister of State at the Home Office in charge of prisons. Two weeks later she was administering punishment to him, delivering death by a thousand cuts. In an appropriately Karloffian metaphor she announced 'there is something of the night about his personality' and unleashed a withering attack. He never recovered and came bottom of the poll. She admitted to 'a chill in the feet' about what she did but never wavered from her determination to administer the *coup de grâce*.

In the words of one Tory former Minister: 'It's been a bull-fight where the bull gets handbagged to death before the sword leaves the scabbard.' In the light of all this it is surprising to discover that she had previously urged parents to boycott a highly successful video game called Mortal Kombat, in one of whose scenes a character called Sub-Zero rips off a head, revealing dangling spinal cord and dripping blood.

Ann's opinions vary from robust to implacable. As she says: 'There has to be something in your life you're prepared to go to the stake for . . . I distrust MPs without causes.' When she recently became a Roman Catholic, following the Church of England's move to ordain women priests, she took the confirmation name of Hugh, after St Hugh of Lincoln and in remembrance of Bishop Latimer who was burnt at the stake in 1555. His last unrepentant words were: 'We shall this day light such candle by God's grace in England as shall never be put out.'

She is sick of the 'self-pitying attitudes of some women MPs' and sees herself exactly on a par with the men in Parliament. She feels she gets on better with, and prefers the company of men to women and some of her worst problems have been caused by women, both in and outside the House. An interviewer recently observed presciently: 'If she were a man she would probably be loved by the British public.'

Her first major battles in Parliament were in the anti-abortion campaign. This earned her this tribute from a left-wing opponent: 'She was the most extreme reactionary in her attitude to women generally. She often takes the hard-line anti-woman line. She has neither sympathy, compassion nor empathy for women.'

She would undoubtedly respond robustly to this attack with her favourite words 'absolute bunkum' or 'rot'. She has, in fact, shown sympathy for women. In 1989 she attacked a judge for sentencing a woman to 30 months in jail for pouring boiling water over the crotch of a man who had raped her five-year-old daughter.

Her absolutism and inner strength were fostered by her school experience. Although her parents were Anglicans she was sent to a very strict RC convent school in Bath. She recalls the regime which she endured right up to the age of 18:

'It was pre-Vatican II: Latin Mass, priest with his back to the people, mortal sin to eat meat on Friday, bed at 7.30 on Saturdays, up at 6.30 to go to Mass. Sunday walks in our Sunday hats in a formal crocodile. We got order marks if seen outside the grounds without our gloves on. It was a bygone age.'

Now she says that she gives 'thanks to Almighty God for the authoritarian element. To have a church which calls a sin a sin and has done with it is a blessed relief.'

She is in favour of capital punishment and supports sending young offenders to military-style 'glasshouses' to learn discipline. She was a vigorous campaigner for nuclear weapons in the Thatcher years. Someone close to her was reported as saying: 'If she were Secretary of State for Defence she'd be in the tank driving into Bosnia. She has an air of Margaret (Thatcher) in her; there's a great deal of similarity.'

She does not allow the comparison to be taken too far: 'I know I haven't a hope of being like Mrs Thatcher. I used to say that Mrs Thatcher could get off a train at five in the morning looking as if she had stepped from a beauty parlour, and I could step out of a beauty parlour and look as though I'd got off a train at five in the morning.'

Underneath the armour-plating she is an affectionate, compassionate friend, generous, kind and unstuffy. Michael Forsyth, then a fellow Home Office Minister, was once horrified to hear her civil servants address her informally as 'Ann' rather than the traditional 'Minister'.

Forsyth, accompanied for moral support by fellow frontbencher Lord Henley, approached Miss Widdecombe to try and talk her round. 'You must be called Minister,' Forsyth urged. Miss Widdecombe would have none of it and declared, 'But God calls me Ann.' Henley countered, 'Well God calls me Lord Henley.' But even this did not win the day and the two Ministers retired defeated.

Ann has a sense of humour and can laugh loudly at herself. On a visit to Askham Grange women's prison she toured the mother and baby unit. Admiring tiny baby Howard, asleep in his pram, she asked his mother mischievously; 'Did you name him after the Home Secretary?'

In spite of lapses, she has maintained her fearsome reputation.

When, in 1991, a survey showed one in five families going hungry she suggested that, since four in five were not, hungry families might be mismanaging things. Some time later she was wheeled out to support, with unrelenting vigour, the Government's policy of shackling pregnant prisoners to hospital beds.

In today's world of spin doctors and media-massaging her forthrightness is refreshing. She was an excellent Minister, master of her brief and fearless in debate. She took it as a mark of respect when, as she rose to make a speech in the House, left-wing Labour MP, Terry Lewis, shouted 'Make it quick, your broomstick's been clamped.'

Following her involuntary move to the Opposition Benches, Ann began a second career as a media star, with 'makeovers' in the tabloids and participation on prime-time television. The public took her to their hearts – with no airs and graces she was a welcome antidote to the silicone-enhanced bimbos who take up far too much air time and column inches. Her media career was interrupted in May 1998 when, not surprisingly, she was promoted to the Shadow Cabinet to 'Duff up Dobbo', the lacklustre Frank Dobson at health. Poor lad, he has no chance.

Margot Asquith
(b.1864 – d.1945)

'She was so talkative and said so much on so many subjects, that
she could hardly avoid saying something good sometimes about
something.'

*****

Margot's father, Sir Charles Tennant, was born in 1823 and made a vast fortune out of property, securities, and gold and diamond mining in South Africa in the freebooting days of mid-Victorian England. At 21 his father had sent him to London from Scotland with a capital of £2000 and an allowance of £400 a year. By the age of 30 he was a millionaire.

He was a man of exceptional vitality. Margot was born in 1864, the eleventh of twelve children by his first marriage. At the age of 75 he married again and sired three more daughters. The second of these last three, Katherine (Baroness Elliott of Harewood), was born in 1903 and survived until January 1994.

At the end of the twentieth century Katherine was able to say three remarkable things – that her grandfather had been born in the eighteenth century; that her father had been born 170 years before; and that she was the sister-in-law of the last Prime Minister of King Edward VII.

This last distinction arose because her half-sister, Margot, had married H.H. Asquith in 1894 and moved to 10 Downing Street in

1908. Margot was at the centre of political and intellectual Society life from the 1880s to the 1920s. She launched forth on the world of fashion, took it by storm and was renowned for her unconventional outspokenness.

As a young woman with almost no formal education she had, nevertheless, been able to captivate one of the learned giants of his day, Dr Benjamin Jowett, Regius Professor of Greek and Master of Balliol College, Oxford. Jowett was silent by nature but this did not matter because Margot's conversation resembled the Niagara Falls in full spate.

Critics said that Margot had no art of conversation. She simply upturned the contents of her mind on whomever she was with and, while these contents could be very interesting, they sometimes consisted of a wearisome name-dropping gabble. However, it is difficult to see how she could have retained the interest of towering intellectuals like Jowett if this had been a fair judgement.

Jowett was only one of her intellectual conquests. Arthur Balfour, not only a philosopher but a Minister for much of the period from 1885-1929 (including three years as Prime Minister) was a devoted member of her circle. She suggested to him that he was so self-contained he would not mind if all his close women friends – Lady Elcho, Lady Desborough and herself – were to die. 'I think I should mind if they all died on the same day,' he replied, after a pause for reflection.

It was said she was so talkative and said so much on so many subjects, that she could hardly avoid saying something good sometimes, about something. She had unquenchable vitality, abounding courage and both the desire and capacity to shine, not only in fashionable society but wherever she happened to be. She was forceful and not prone to take 'no' for an answer. Her bossiness sometimes had surprisingly beneficial effects. In 1893 Jowett became seriously ill at the age of 76. While still able to do so, he solemnly composed farewell letters to all his friends, dictating them to his housekeeper. Margot received one but, refusing to take his illness seriously, telegraphed back at once: 'I refuse to accept your farewell letter to me: you have been listening to some silly woman and believing what she says.' The telegram had a magical effect.

From that moment Jowett got steadily better, as instructed.

She was able to hold her own not only with the taciturn but also with formidable talkers like Mr Gladstone. He was delighted with her vivacity and her charm, which she displayed by sitting on his knee as he recited poetry; he was 80 and she was 25 at the time. Exciting the Grand Old Man by her interest, he turned out some laudatory verses about her which will stand comparison with the cream of the great William McGonagle himself:

> *When Parliament ceases and comes the recess*
> *And we seek in the country rest after distress*
> *As a rule upon visitors place an embargo*
> *But make an exception in favour of Margot.*

She married Asquith as his second wife in 1894, when he was already Home Secretary. Fiercely proud and protective of him, regarding him as insufficiently self-assertive, she said 'his modesty amounts almost to deformity'. Margot regarded herself as his second pair of eyes, his most faithful and alert watchdog.

In this respect she did not always win over supporters. Self-criticism was quite alien to her. Her self-conceit was irrepressible but men often found her lack of inhibition alluring. Lord Randolph Churchill asked her, when she first came out in Society, if she knew any politicians. She replied without hesitation that with the exception of himself, she 'knew them all intimately'.

As the wife of the Prime Minister her behaviour would be counted extraordinary if it happened today; before the First World War it was regarded with incredulity. She sometimes bought a 3rd class railway ticket, deliberately, to enable her to engage in conversation with a carriage full of total strangers. Habitually disconcerting the company (especially if any were so discourteous as to read in her presence) she announced her identity and delivered a lecture beginning: 'Now, I am Mrs Asquith and I expect you would like me to tell you something about my husband.'

In the absence of corridors the only escape lay in pulling the communication cord, risking a fine of 40 shillings, which would probably have been cheap at the price. Alas! it cannot now be determined whether the Prime Minister's interests were advanced by Margot's missionary zeal.

Margot did not ruminate overlong on the impact of her actions. Her general view was that popularity mattered not one jot and was generally enjoyed by those who had no strength of character and who always fell in with the wishes of others.

At No 10 Margot was apt to run downstairs, charge headlong into the drawing room without notice, shriek out a welcome, light a cigarette and begin a conversation that could be heard all over the house. She often made acid comments in public about anybody who attracted her antipathy, even members of Asquith's government. She was repeatedly told she ought to be more dignified and circumspect, but this was congenitally impossible.

She had an acid tongue which etched some brilliant turns of phrase:

Winston (Churchill) 'would kill his own mother just to use her skin to make a drum to beat his own praises'.

Lloyd George 'could not see a belt without hitting below it'.

F.E. Smith 'is very clever but his brains go to his head'.

Sir Stafford Cripps 'has a brilliant mind – until it is made up'.

'If Kitchener was not a great man he was at least a great poster'.

Margot did not like Lord Lonsdale, who was famous for his magnificent horses and his courage in the hunting field. On hearing someone praise his prowess as a rider to hounds, she interjected: 'Jump? Anyone can jump. Look at fleas.'

Her manner, and the ease with which she collected celebrities, often irritated Society competitors. On one occasion an argument developed between a group of fashionable men and women about the merits of a new volume of essays by J A Symonds. Margot criticised their style and content with some gusto. The great Society hostess, Lady Londonderry, nettled either by Margot's opinion or her confident manner, attempted to put her down rather grandly: 'Mrs Asquith, I am afraid you have not read the book.' Margot later recalled her devastating reply: 'This annoyed me . . . I thought it unnecessarily rude and more than foolish. I looked at her calmly and said "I am afraid, Lady Londonderry, you have not read the Preface. The book is dedicated to me."'

She looked on herself as a percipient critic of politics but was, in fact, almost devoid of political judgment. However, she did occasionally manipulate her extensive contacts to some advantage. On 2 August 1914, two days before war was declared, she wrote to John Redmond, the leader of the Irish Nationalist Party, asking him to set an example of patriotism by making a speech in support of the government. The very next day in the House of Commons Redmond assured the government that they could safely withdraw troops from Ireland for redeployment against Germany and that 'armed Nationalist Catholics in the south would be glad to join armed Protestant Ulstermen in the north'.

Surprisingly Margot did not admire women in politics, observing, 'No amount of education will make women first-rate politicians. Can you see a woman becoming a Prime Minister? I cannot imagine a greater calamity for these islands than to be under the guidance of a woman in 10 Downing Street.' Clearly, she would have got on famously with Sir Edward Heath.

She appeared to lack systematic thought, but her unstructured mind compensated by provoking thoughts in others by means of colourful phrases and unexpected associations. She told Lord David Cecil: 'Lord Dawson was not a good doctor. King George V himself told me that he would never have died had he had another doctor.'

Her step-daughter, Violet, asked if she would wear a particular hat trimmed with ostrich feathers to Lord Kitchener's memorial service. She replied, 'My dear, how can you possibly ask me? Dear Kitchener saw me in that hat twice.'

Margot could be acerbic as well as dotty. When Jean Harlow, the platinum blonde 1930s movie star, met Lady Asquith for the very first time, she made the *faux pas* of addressing her familiarly by her Christian name. She compounded the error by pronouncing 'Margot' to rhyme with 'rot'. Lady Asquith cuttingly corrected her: 'My dear, the "t" is silent as in Harlow.'

Her daughter, Elizabeth, impulsively fell in love with a young and impecunious American diplomat. Margot's reaction was not favourable and she did all she could to discourage the match: 'To marry an American is bad enough, but a poor American! This is really too much.' The marriage did not take place.

However, she did not always get the better of Americans. Dorothy Parker, whose tongue was even sharper, reviewed her book *Lay Sermons* in the *New Yorker*.

'"Daddy, what's an optimist?" said Pat to Mike while they were walking down the street together one day. "One who thought that M. Asquith wasn't going to write any more," replied the absent-minded professor, as he wound up the cat and put the clock out. That gifted entertainer, the Countess of Oxford and Asquith, author of *The Autobiography of Margot Asquith* (four volumes, ready boxed suitable for throwing purposes), reverts to tripe in a new book deftly entitled *Lay Sermons*.

In this book of essays, which has all the depth and glitter of a worn dime, the Countess walks right up to such subjects as Health, Human Nature, Fame, Character, Marriage, Politics and Opportunities. Successively, she knocks down and drags out each topic. And there is something vastly stirring in the way in which, no matter where she takes off from, she brings the discourse back to Margot Asquith. Such singleness of purpose is met but infrequently . . .

The affair between M. Asquith and M. Asquith will live as one of the prettiest love stories in all history.'

Margot was striking but not pretty. She said of herself, 'I haven't got a face – I have two profiles.' Perhaps because of this, Margot always felt a little precarious. She knew that Asquith was notoriously, if platonically, susceptible to intelligent young women. He conducted a long-running affair with Venetia Stanley, even writing long and wildly indiscreet letters to her during Cabinet meetings. This was dangerous stuff, even in the days long before editors induced the public to keep taking the tabloids by publishing long-range photographs of the oral pedicure of princesses.

But although Margot was a supreme Battleaxe in defence of

Asquith against his detractors, she was indulgently tolerant of his personal foibles: 'No woman should expect to be the only woman in her husband's life . . . I not only encouraged his female friends but posted his letters to them if I found them in our front hall.' Asquith's affairs were harmless enough in an age when libidos often burst their superficial strait-laces. Sir Charles Dilke MP, on his second night staying in the Tennant house, met Laura (Margot's younger sister) in a passageway on her way to bed. He tried a rather unusual chat-up line: 'If you will kiss me I will give you a signed photograph.' Laura displayed the presence of mind which was the hallmark of the Tennant girls: 'It is awfully good of you, Sir Charles, but I would rather not, for what on earth would I do with the photograph?'

As his responsibilities in office increased, Asquith directly increased his intake of alcohol. A C Benson noted one night's performance at the National Liberal Club (which did not enjoy a reputation as a temple of self-indulgence): 'He ate, drank and smoked deep – 5 or 6 cigars, much champagne, port or liqueurs.' Margot, at one point, decided to act as any self-respecting Battleaxe should; she started to water the brandy decanter. However, Asquith quickly twigged this stratagem and took the necessary counter-action.

In December 1916 Asquith was forced out of the premiership. One cause of Asquith's unpopularity was the leaking of a secret memorandum from Lord Lansdowne advocating peace negotiations. Margot's reaction was emphatically Battleaxey. The following year, referring to new peace feelers, she wrote to the *Daily Telegraph*, 'Peace now makes me shudder. In my days in Downing St we never heard the word mentioned. War in our day meant that the Germans were to be brought to their knees.'

Margot was equally intransigent in her refusal to accept the finality of Asquith's ejection. In spite of her announcement that 'we mean to live quietly, only seeing the King and a few friends', she fought like a tigress to reinstate him. She never forgot the humiliation nor did she forgive those she held principally responsible.

Ann Gloag

Ann Gloag

'Predatory, deplorable and against the public interest.'
(Monopolies and Mergers Commission comment on one of her
proposed takeovers)
*****

Ann Gloag is a Battlebus, the vehicular equivalent of the Battleaxe. She is one of the most successful female entrepreneurs in British history. The daughter of a humble bus driver, she now owns a sizeable proportion of Britain's bus and railway fleet, together with companies in Malawi, Kenya, Hong Kong, New Zealand and Portugal. In 15 years she rose from nothing to become the second richest woman in Britain after the Queen.

She has not achieved this transformation by sitting on her rear assets. She is an entrepreneur to her fingertips and took instant advantage of the deregulation of Britain's bus industry. As Britain's most aggressive bus group, Stagecoach has been subject to more referrals to the Monopolies and Mergers Commission than any other company. One of the suggested names for the company was 'Blunderbus' which seems singularly appropriate to describe the way the company blitzed every competitor in sight.

Born in 1942, Ann grew up in a council house in Perth. In 1995 she paid £2.8 million for Beaufort Castle and its contents, for over 500 years the seat of one of Scotland's most historic families, the Frasers of Lovat. It is a fairytale, turreted folly nestling on the banks of the river Beauly in Inverness-shire. She explained, 'I had to buy it. All the other bidders were from abroad.' A far cry from her humble origins, but she lives more modestly near Perth and uses the magnificent castle, with its 24 bedrooms and private chapel, merely for company entertaining and during school holidays.

Ann started work as a nurse at Perth Infirmary, rising to become a theatre sister. Close observation of surgeons taking slices from the bodies of patients enabled her to learn the techniques with which she has neatly sliced up her business competitors ever since.

When she was just 18 she married Robin Gloag only a matter of months after he had limped into her hospital with a torn cartilage. He was a petrol station manager. 'We were always hard up and I always knew I would have to be the breadwinner,' she said. She was soon running a business from home, hiring out caravans and minibuses as a sideline to nursing, to help out the family finances, by then stretched with the arrival of two children.

In 1980 she and her brother Brian founded a company called Stagecoach, using their father's £25,000 redundancy money, plus some money from an uncle in Canada, as working capital. She and her husband gave up their jobs and her brother moved into their house, putting every penny they had into the business.

They started with a single route from Dundee to London. Their fares were half those of the competition. Robin was the driver whilst Ann and her mother made the sandwiches, tea and shortbread which were sold on board.

By aggressive expansion in the 'bus-wars' following deregulation in the 1980s, Stagecoach became Europe's biggest bus company and the most successful in Britain, controlling more than a quarter of the country's bus routes.

Ann's rapid rise to riches has been controversial. Many regard her as a vicious and ruthless operator. The Monopolies Commission has attacked her business practices as 'predatory, deplorable and against the public interest'.

There have been many acquisitions along the way but there have also been disposals – not least Ann Gloag's first husband, Robin. As the company went from strength to strength their marriage withered and died.

In 1983 Ann and Brian called Robin to a meeting and told him they wanted to buy him out. Robin was given two buses and £8000 as his share of the business. He set up a bus company plying between Perth and Errol, a journey of 15 minutes. The service operated as a rival to Stagecoach and was called Highwayman.

Alas poor Robin! He quickly found the normal roles reversed and, for the first time ever, the Highwayman was held up at gunpoint by the Stagecoach. For daring to compete, Ann determined to put him out of business. When he cut his fares from £1 to 80p she cut hers to 50p. When he followed suit she slashed her fares to zero and allowed people to travel for free. Robin quickly pulled onto the hard shoulder and gave up the unequal struggle. He went bust and she bought the mangled wreckage.

Ann says of this episode, 'It makes me sound awful, but I can't deny it's the truth.' Robin's response is prosaic: ' Money was always everything to her and she's good at making it. I wish the story would die and them with it.' He still holds one Stagecoach share which they tried to prise from him but he would not sign. 'They didn't push hard enough and I didn't fall off the cliff.'

Ann had more in common with brother Brian, although their styles could not be more different. She dresses well (although professes still to buy her clothes from the same shops she used when a nurse) and uses the normal female sartorial weapons of castellated shoulder pads. By contrast, Brian surprised, indeed shocked, the staid members of the Commons Select Committee on Transport by turning up to give evidence to them in open necked shirt and trainers.

Her acumen converted the original 1980 investment of £25,000 into £134 million when Stagecoach floated on the Stock Market in 1993. It is now worth many times more. She knows how to spot a good deal and shake up dozy businesses. If she can't cut a deal she will cut throats.

In 1994 Darlington Borough Council decided to sell its bus operation. Stagecoach put in a bid but rival company Yorkshire Traction emerged as the preferred bidder. Not to be outdone, Stagecoach first lured away Darlington's drivers with £1000 bonuses. Then they administered the *coup de grâce* by running a rival service two minutes ahead of the competition – entirely free of charge. Yorkshire withdrew its bid. Darlington failed to find another buyer. Darlington's bus company went bust and Stagecoach inherited their business!

Ann explains her success very simply. 'I have the ability to negotiate. Whether it is with £2 in the fish market or £2 million, the principle is the same. I make tremendous deals. Just plain common sense.'

Others are less kind. In the words of a local businessman: 'She's a stuck-up asset stripper, a couldn't-care-less capitalist who could sink someone with a small business like me – she'd fight you down to the last penny.'

Gloag has a formidable reputation. The 'Gloag Stare' is feared in the City. 'You don't see the bullet until it hits you,' says one City analyst. Only 5 feet tall, she proves the old adage that dynamite comes in small packs. In 1990 Ann was Veuve Cliquot Business-woman of the Year although, being teetotal, perhaps she should have been disqualified from consideration.

She does not now court publicity. She was incandescent when a *World in Action* crew took a helicopter ride over Beaufort Castle and solicitors' letters flew to Granada. When she heard the BBC were planning a film about her operations which criticised her business practice, she spent £70,000 on newspaper advertising, taunting them with the headline: 'We'll take the high road while they take the low road.'

Ann has strong religious beliefs and is an evangelical Christian. Quietly, without the attendant publicity which many celebrities and millionaires seek, she is a generous giver to charitable causes, in particular in the third world. For example, in memory of her previous life in the burns unit of a hospital, she has set up a burns ward in the Queen Elizabeth Hospital in the capital of Malawi, where she is the largest bus operator. She funds an orphanage in Nairobi, having previously adopted a Kenyan boy, Peter, who now lives in the extended family of Ann, her second husband and their 'his 'n' hers' children.

Not only does she have her head screwed on for business, but she is also determined that her children should know the value of money and not take a multi-millionairess mother for granted. Her children work for their money and she kept her son, Jonathan, so financially constrained while at university that he had to drive a bus at weekends to make ends meet. Her daughter also has a bus driver's licence in case the family fall on hard times.

Ann staunchly defends her achievements and her wealth; 'I worked very hard for it. When people achieve success we should praise and cherish them.'

Barbara Woodhouse

Barbara Woodhouse
(b. 1910 – d. 1988)

'It's the owners who need to be trained, not the dogs'
*****

'Dr Doolittle in tweeds' was how one obituarist summed up the stentorian-voiced, commanding animal trainer, Barbara Wood-house. 'It's the owners who need to be trained, not the dogs' was a typical no-nonsense piece of Woodhouse wisdom. She firmly believed that 'the average dog is far more intelligent than the average child'.

The age and fitness of the owner was more important than that of the dog on a Woodhousian training weekend – which resembled an army assault course. Owners had to bend down quickly many times, run, walk and jump, often in boiling sun. 'Dawdlers don't make good dog handlers,' she declaimed.

Barbara was born in 1910 in a boys' prep school near Dublin where her father was headmaster until he died when she was aged nine. 'Why can't Barbara be beautiful like the other children,' her mother wailed. From that moment on, as 'they didn't seem to mind what I looked like,' Barbara preferred the company of dogs and men; strictly in that order of priority.

In later life she took umbrage at being described as an 'amorphous mass' and as a size 18. Janet Brown, the female impressionist, had huge difficulty in 'coping with that great bosom which moves very happily around by itself inside her jumper'.

She left school at 16 'never having learned anything that could, in my opinion, be of any use to me. Every mistress had disliked me because I always smelled strongly of horses.'

In the 1930s she went to the Argentine and worked with 120 men and 600 horses, learning the old Indian trick of blowing into a horse's nose to effect an introduction in the process of taming. History does not relate whether she tamed the Argentine men in similar fashion.

Animals always, quite properly, took priority. When soap flakes were scarce during the war, the babies' nappies frequently went unwashed, but never did she miss washing the tails of the cows, brushing them out into thick bushes.

She first hit the headlines in 1950 for slapping a man in her home village of Croxley Green. 'I would like to make it absolutely clear that it had nothing to do with the dancing on the common or the parking of cars or the setting up the arena. It was simply because of what the man said to me.' What she said is, sadly, unrecorded but the man in question had called her a 'bloody autocrat', to which she took autocratic exception.

Mrs Woodhouse brought to heel a world record 17,000 dogs and even the Royal corgis did not escape her barbs: 'I have seen them waiting on a station platform exhibiting dreadful impatience.'

She trained her own Great Dane, Juno, to do all manner of useful things – to pull the children's bedclothes off, vacuum the sitting room and answer the telephone. At the sound of the telephone bell, the dog would lift the receiver, give a short acknowledging bark, and fetch his mistress. Juno also had to bark when the milk boiled over and sit in a queue moving Barbara's basket along with her mouth when the queue moved.

Juno became a celebrated matinée idol, starring in all manner of films and enjoying all the trappings of stardom; being taken to the studio by Rolls-Royce and given publicity like one of her human co-stars. Juno was offered half a million pounds to go to the US to star in 69 episodes of a series specially written for her. But Barbara could not accept this: 'My beloved dog would be absolutely miserable if she had to leave me.'

With her woollen jersey, tartan tweed skirt, sensible shoes and trademark cry of 'Walkies!' she had total self-confidence when dealing with animals. She reckoned to make any dog obedient to her (but not necessarily its owner) within two or, at the very outside, six minutes.

Often, when handed back to their owners, the dogs behaved very badly, demonstrating to Barbara's satisfaction that it was the owners at fault, not the dogs. 'If you don't get it into the owners' heads, how can you expect the dogs to understand? Unless a dog is born bonkers, there is no such thing as a bad dog, only bad owners.'

For dogs who chase cars, Mrs Woodhouse believed in the short sharp shock. A car driven by someone other than the owner of the dog would drive slowly past the delinquent canine. As it came to attack the car a heavy book (she suggested the AA manual) should be thrown firmly at the dog, making sure it hit him, while the owner remained concealed. This treatment was 'infallible' and never had to be repeated more than twice.

Her enduring best seller *Talking to Animals* was written in only five days in 1954. Following this, she became a great globetrotter, promoting her ideas and her books from New Zealand and Australia to America, South Africa and most points in between.

She taught herself German in a matter of weeks in order to be interviewed for half-an-hour on German television in their native language. Perhaps her extraordinary facility with German is explained by Frederick the Great's remark that he spoke Latin to God, French to his mistress and German to his horse! On the morning of the programme she rose at 5.00 a.m. to milk the cows and exercise the dogs before flying to Hamburg to do the TV programme. She returned the next morning in time to milk the cows again!

In 1981 she flew to Washington by Concorde for just 48 hours as guest of Bobby Kennedy's widow, Ethel, to be the star attraction at her annual charity dog show. 'The family have 11 children and 9 dogs, all completely untrained and wandering in and out of the house at will. I didn't have time to train them all but gave a couple of the children and dogs the six-minute routine and they will pass it on to the rest. Lovely family, so polite.'

Her first abiding passion was cars, 'I just love them'. She was a rally driver and tuned all the cars in the area. She lectured on road safety to thousands of school children but gave up in 1961 after losing her appeal against conviction for failing to stop her van for a school crossing patrol. She claimed it would have been unsafe to stop because of the wet conditions. 'I am an absolute fiend for paying attention and I lecture on road safety. I am finished with road safety now. My Great Dane, Juno, died last Saturday and now this. It is too much.'

So fearsome was her reputation that employees at British Leyland leapt from the windows to escape when she turned up at Coventry with car problems. She knew, probably more than they did, what went on under a bonnet and, more importantly, how to deal with recalcitrant men and dogs.

She was physically irrepressible. In 1981 she said 'I don't think I do badly for 71. Most people of my age are wearing lace caps and dribbling in old people's homes.' Three years later she suffered a stroke, but even that did not break her indomitable spirit. She was able to speak only very slowly but nevertheless still took thirty to forty calls a day from dog owners.

She eventually heard her own command 'Sit and Down' in July 1988 and went to the Great Dogs' Home in the sky. Before departing she observed, 'I can't believe there is a heaven without animals.'

Edwina Currie

'I'm as tough inside as I am outside.'
*****

Edwina Currie (née Cohen) is a curious mixture of the orthodox and unorthodox. Her father was the same – simultaneously an orthodox Jew and an atheist. In this paradoxical position he resembled Enoch Powell, who once declared himself to be 'an Anglican atheist. I think nothing of religion, but I think there ought to be an established Church and the King of England ought to be its Head.' Edwina's father compounded the paradox by also being anti-Zionist – according to Edwina he thought the creation of the State of Israel a 'batty' idea.

She rejected Jewish orthodoxy in two ways. First, she thought the dietary laws were stupid: 'I wanted a more profound philosophy than one that said you can't have butter on your bread if you're having a meat dinner.' Secondly, in her mid-20s she married a Gentile, following which her father refused to see or speak to her ever again.

Named after Edwina Mountbatten, she grew up in an argumentative household. One suspects that this would have been so even if she had been the only resident. She was always interested in politics and admits to being 'an articulate, argumentative and stubborn child . . . known as Awkward Emma.' This soubriquet may unwittingly provide an insight into her personality. Jane Austen's Emma was a clever, pretty, self-satisfied girl whose sometimes unlikely schemes led in the end to considerable mortification.

Edwina attended the Liverpool Institute for Girls and became Deputy Head Girl. She says she would have become Head Girl but for being Jewish. We can believe this, for Edwina is a true Battleaxe and, if she sets her mind to achieve something that is possible, only an insurmountable external obstacle will prevent it.

Her father was a tailor and socialist trade union activist in Liverpool. She loved to argue with him and thus talked herself into a centre-right position which, among Liverpool teenagers in the 1960s, was unusual – unlike today, when it would be almost inconceivable, Scouse Conservatives being now an endangered species.

Knowing that nothing succeeds like excess, she first came to prominence by waving handcuffs in the air while making a Law and Order speech in 1981 to an orgasmic Conservative Conference. Lord Gowrie, then a Cabinet Minister, confessed to having felt 'a bat's squeak of desire' for her. Years later, in April 1992, John Major offered her the job of Prisons Minister which would have brought her back into the political mainstream following her hasty exit after the salmonella-in-eggs fiasco. Unfortunately for Michael Howard, she turned it down and it went to Ann Widdecombe, whose attacks on his dealings with the head of the Prison Service scuppered his chances of the Tory leadership.

Apparently obsessed by sex, she clearly regards herself as a kind of middle-aged sex bomb. Always banging on about banging away, she never misses a chance to talk about her sexy underwear or comment on other people's sex lives (complete with helpful hints) and used to refer to her converted windmill in Derbyshire as 'penis shaped'. When asked how she stays young and in trim she replies, 'Sex – and weight training in the Commons gym.' It is not clear whether we are meant to connect the activities, but no doubt a future novel will reveal all. When asked who was the sexiest male MP she told an interviewer, 'David Alton. He's so sweet.' At the time Alton was a celibate. No doubt spurred on by Edwina's expression of interest, he quickly married.

She enjoys the effect she thinks she has on men. 'I find it easier to be interviewed by blokes,' she says, 'I can make them squirm.' Men do, of course, 'squirm' for many different reasons.

Sir Nicholas Fairbairn MP made his view of her very clear during a Commons debate on fluoride. He was inveighing against fluoridation of drinking water, arguing that fluoride is 'a potent catalase poison.' Edwina interjected, 'Anything is a poison if we take enough of it. Were we to spread-eagle my Hon. friend on the floor of the House and pour absolutely pure water into him, it would kill him in hours.' It was Sir Nicholas who did the flooring by responding, 'All the poison that she suggested I would happily take, rather than be spread-eagled on the floor of the House by her.'

Ken Livingstone reportedly turned down the opportunity to earn a quick £25,000 to appear in a television advert with her because he would have been obliged to kiss her. If this was so, one can only wonder what sum might have tempted him away from his newts.

She is the only person who admits to having telephoned the satirical TV programme *Spitting Image* complaining that she had not been featured. Her wish was instantly granted with the appearance of a grotesque puppet resembling a cross between Cruella de Ville and a witch from *Macbeth*. Some critics thought this made Edwina the odd-man-out on the programme, all the other characters being caricatures. Edwina cheerfully noted: 'There was a mad look in my eyes which my friends recognised. At first I was shocked but in retrospect it was fairly accurate. The worst thing would have been not to be on at all.'

'Satire is part of democracy' she said, mourning the show's passing, 'it has a way of keeping politicians from taking themselves too seriously.' She blamed the politicians for the show's demise, 'Politicians have learned to be bland. It's very difficult to take people off when they are all the same. Blair and Major are not the stuff of great comedy.'

Regardless of any faults, she is a good sport and can laugh at herself. She tells a tale about opening a new ward at a hospital in Birmingham, when she was junior Health Minister. Halfway through her speech a psychiatric patient started shouting at her 'You're bananas. You're talking absolute poppycock.' Edwina inquired whether the patient was unwell. 'Good heavens, no!' said Matron. 'He's been here for 15 years and it's the first time he's talked sense.'

She is crack-crazy on publicity, 'making Jeffrey Archer look like a recluse', according to one MP. She admits to having sought constant local publicity for the routine acts which every MP performs day in and day out – helping elderly ladies with their sewage problems, for example. She says 'What's the good of doing good by stealth', as if 'doing good' is worthless unless illuminated by a blaze of publicity. Being instantly recognizable has not been in vain. She put it to good use once in dealing with a traffic warden in Bristol. Nipping into a bank, she left her car on double yellow lines and returned just as she was about to be booked. Apparently, she so charmed the traffic warden that he forgot to issue a ticket.

But, in a publicity coup to eclipse all others, she announced during a tour to promote her latest book, *She's Leaving Home*, that she was leaving home and her long-suffering husband, Ray. Nobody else was involved in the break-up so one can only conclude that, after serving twenty-five years of his life sentence, Ray had been granted parole due to good behaviour.

Her first room mate at the Commons was the late Richard Holt MP, also newly elected in 1983. He complained of having to suffer her interminable self-publicizing down the telephone all day long but he was also an obvious target for nagging, being a drinker, a smoker and considerably overweight. He described her as 'to the Tory Party what the Bishop of Durham is to the Church of England', and it was only a matter of weeks before he could stand it no longer and begged the Whips to move him – anywhere, but preferably to the opposite end of the Palace of Westminster.

She was promoted early by Margaret Thatcher, perhaps inspiring a touch of envy amongst some of her male colleagues for her 'ball-breaking chutzpah'. While they fought for little mentions in their local press, Edwina was strutting through the nationals day in and day out. Colleagues queued up to say unfriendly things about her. Andrew Mackay MP remarked that she had 'done for our Party what King Herod did for babysitting'. Frank Dobson MP, now Secretary of State for Health, gibed, 'When she goes to the dentist, he's the one who needs the anaesthetic.'

Equally outspoken about her colleagues, Edwina claimed the three occupational hazards of politicians are Arrogance, Alcohol and Adultery. She is right but admits to falling foul of only one personally.

Nicknamed 'Vindaloo', she inspired a group of overweight, chip-loving, beer-swilling Tory MPs to form The Currie Club. They met regularly to eat a hugely unhealthy cholesterol-saturated meal as a protest against her meddling bossy ways. At Christmas, their general feeling was that it would be preferable to hang her and kiss the mistletoe. They also expressed the view that 'She's the kind of person who gives people something to live for – revenge.'

In spite of her rejection of what she regarded as Jewish food fads, as junior Health Minister she had a mania for imposing her own particular fads on the entire country in the name of the new religion of 'food fascism'. In 1988 she resigned from her job over the salmonella-in-eggs débâcle.

A colleague shrewdly assessed the situation by saying, 'Eggs are less dangerous than some politicians.' Eggwina's remark that 'We do warn people now that most of the egg production in this country, sadly, is now infected with salmonella', triggered an immediate slump in consumption with catastrophic consequences for the egg industry. As reported in Teresa Gorman's *Chickengate*, published by the Institute of Economic Affairs, within a matter of days egg consumption fell by 50 per cent overall and, in hospitals and schools, by 90 per cent, the eventual cost to the taxpayer being in excess of £70,000,000. Years later, when challenged to admit that she might, just once, have got something wrong politically, she retorted, 'There's never been any point.'

She is similarly coy about possible personal failings. 'She's so conceited she has her x-rays re-touched,' said one colleague. Of herself, she says, 'If I had wanted to change something, I would have. I'm content.' Having said that, she has recently had a 'nose job' but, of course, the original nose was Mother Nature's fault, not hers. 'I'd look like Elle Macpherson if I could. But, on the whole, I'd rather keep my brains.'

Described by a male interviewer as 'the most astonishingly bossy woman I have ever met' and by a female colleague as 'a sanctimonious nagger', Edwina delights in telling the rest of us how best we should live our lives. The eggs fiasco was just one example. Pensioners were also briskly instructed to knit their own central heating in the form of woolly hats and gloves. The poor were lectured on the deficiencies of their diet.

'She may be thoughtless but she's never speechless.' She shoots from the lip and once spoke too incautiously when delivering an insult to Dennis Skinner, a fellow Derbyshire MP. 'Derbyshire born, Derbyshire bred, strong of arm, thick of head.' That was fine; it insulted Mr Skinner – although, of course, the insult could not penetrate very far. But Edwina forgot that many of her own Derbyshire constituents might not have appreciated her description of their alleged common characteristics.

Edwina is clever and is certainly nobody's fool. She is intensely resilient and versatile. Politics having gone sour for her, she turned her capable hand to writing. There is no denying that her books sell and she is now an immensely successful writer, having just published her third novel. She is aware of Sam Goldwyn's insight that no one ever lost money underestimating public taste. She says she is 'not a very sophisticated person' and that explains why she enjoys her own novels.

She was unflatteringly summed up in an interview by Lynn Barber: 'Despite her Oxford education, her high flying career, her media celebrity, she still behaves like a pushy provincial hair-saloniste queening it over her fellow passengers on a SAGA cruise to Tenerife.'

But Edwina doesn't care what people think although she knows the effect she has on many. When she was Parliamentary Slimmer of the Year in 1993 she said, 'I have lost 10 per cent of my body weight, so there is 10 per cent less of me to annoy people.' Edwina's skin is 'armour plated, bullet proof and missile-resistant'. She is unlike many of the Battleaxes in the book who are more vulnerable than they appear. As she says herself, 'I'm as tough inside as I am outside.'

Karren Brady

'I've got to do eight things at a time or I get bored. Everything's always got to be done yesterday and there's always a solution to problems.'

*****

Karren Brady is tough. She can't remember the last time she was frightened.

When she was 19 a burglar broke into her house and lay in wait until she arrived home. Hitting her in the face, he grabbed her handbag and drove off with it. Undaunted, she jumped into her car, gave chase, cornered him in a cul-de-sac and demanded her bag back. When he refused, she grabbed a flask from the back seat of his car and hit him repeatedly over the head with it, while being dragged under his car as he tried to reverse at full speed. Startled by this Amazonian display, he then produced a knife. Karren pretended to give up but caught him unawares and nipped off at speed with her bag intact.

She left school with four good 'A' levels but rejected the 'Cup-a-Soup life' of university, preferring to 'get rich quick' instead. At an interview for a junior executive's job with Saatchi and Saatchi she was asked whether she would prefer a designer coat or one from M&S. Her response 'It depends who's paying', secured her the job.

Karren (her name is spelled with two 'r's because it rhymes with Darren and her mother thought that was the way it was) is a classic high achiever. 'I'm like my Dad. I've got to do eight things at a time or I get bored. Everything's always got to be done yesterday, and there's always solutions to problems.'

She has hinted at going into politics. 'I could really kick ass in politics.' Her role model, of course, is Margaret Thatcher. John Major did not impress: 'He's such a plonker.'

Karren has always had goals. Now she concentrates on two in particular – at either end of Birmingham City's football ground where she calls the shots as Managing Director. She was installed there by 'Sultan of Smut' David Sullivan, the Club's co-owner.

The 'porn again' multi-millionaire spotted her drive and ability straight away. On her first day selling advertising for LBC radio, she decided to ginger up clients who had not spent much on advertising. Sullivan was one such backslider.

Sullivan makes a fortune out of telephone chat lines, but Karren could not get to talk to him. Having failed to pierce the secretarial defences at his office, she turned up on the doorstep at his home. At first he was furious but her audacity impressed him and he gave her five minutes to make her case. She persuaded him to spend £2 million on radio advertising within the next two months and his sales soared. This was just as well, as she gave him a money-back guarantee, without the means to pay if she was wrong.

Sullivan liked her 'tough as nails' attitude so much that he poached her to become Sales & Marketing Director of his 'tit and bum' paper the *Sport*. As the 57th richest man in Britain, Sullivan was looking for new ways to spend. He bought Birmingham City jointly with the Gold brothers for £2 million in 1993, for something to do on a Saturday afternoon, and installed Karren as Managing Director aged 25. The Club was instantly nicknamed 'Bummingham Titty'.

Birmingham City was just another way of saying 'problems'. As Karren said soon after taking over: 'Everything you look at in Birmingham is negative. Anything you thought was bad, when you look into it, it's worse.'

Working a fifteen-hour day, she demanded to be regarded and treated as an equal by visiting male Managing Directors, many of whom could not cope with battling Brady and her aggressive ways. Brady achieved staggering success. She reduced a mountain of debt, sacked all but two members of staff (they hid in the locker room to escape and were overlooked) changed the strip back to blue and white (posing in it provocatively for the local press, thus ensuring a sell-out), re-built the ground and trebled the gate. The club jumped from the Second to the First Division and traded at a profit for the first time in 120 years.

At first, other football managers, being male, macho and sexist, made the mistake of not taking her seriously. Aston Villa's chairman, Doug Ellis, sat next to her at a sports dinner and, not knowing who she was, kissed her hand, patronised her as 'my darling' and asked who she worked for. When she said 'Birmingham City', he asked 'in which department?', assuming she was referring to the City Council.

Perceived as the bimbo product of a porn empire, rumour and innuendo were rife that she had 'slept' her way into the job. Her response, 'I'm not bonking the boss' shows who would have been in charge if she had been. Rather than resenting the false rumours, she used them to her advantage.

Her reputation in the world of football is legendary, in particular amongst those who cross her on a bad day. She justifies her tough stance – 'Do you want to be everybody's friend or do you want a good club?'

She does not like firing people. 'It is the worst part of the job but I tell them they are not performing, ask them to suggest an alternative, and they can't.' Early on she dismissed footballers as intellectually challenged and 'only interested in drinking, clothes and the size of their willies'.

She has clearly revised her opinion as she married Paul Peschisolido, the Canadian-born striker who arrived at the club shortly after she did and very quickly scored. The *People* newspaper got wind of her affair with Paul and threatened to reveal all. Karren out-gunned them by selling her story to their deadly rival, The *News of the World*, posing for them in her nightie.

The *People* should have twigged that no one crosses Brady and wins. The *Observer*, later claiming all innocence, described her on her arrival at Birmingham City as a Page Three Girl. It was a bigger boob than any printed in the *Sport*. Instant legal action secured a swift and complete climb down.

Many men want her to fail in order to prove their own machismo. They will be disappointed. Her obvious female attractions belie a backbone of steel and some hapless males were caught on the hop in the early days. More interested in scoring with her than the club, one player cheekily made a sexist remark about her cleavage. He was easily dispatched: 'I'll sell you to Crewe and you won't be able to see them from there.'

Women got no special treatment. One paper reported that – faithfully or otherwise – should a member of staff phone in with period pains, 'I would sack them on the spot.' Karren doesn't believe in period pains. Should another request time off because of a sickly child 'I'd think – what a wimp.'

Perhaps, once she has kicked Birmingham City into the Premier League, she could be persuaded to 'kick ass in politics' – she would certainly liven up the Tory Party at Westminster!

Dame Shirley Porter

*'Domineering and difficult to work with, she has a relentlessly
sharp tongue.'*
*****

Shirley Porter is a 'doer'. She went into politics to Get Things Done.
Unfortunately it was she who 'got done' in the end. She had a
ceaseless itch for activity, inherited from her father whose guiding
acronym was YCDBSOYA (You can't do business sitting on your
ass), which she frequently repeated. The dozing devotees of a quiet
life found her 'ruthless and obsessed'. Working for her was a bit like
being chained to a St Vitus' Dance victim.

Shirley was born in Clapton in 1930. Her father, Sir Jack Cohen,
pulled himself up by his bootstraps from barrow boy to
supermarket king. He created his Tesco empire on a simple
philosophy: 'Pile it high, sell it cheap'. He made his millions by
providing good value for the millions. In a retailing revolution he
slashed prices and raised quality – substantially boosting the living
standards of ordinary people in the process.

Jews have always been outsiders – and this has often been a spur
to success in business. Shirley was no exception. She had her first
brush with anti-Semitism while at school in Worthing during the
war. She was bullied but, nevertheless, became a prefect and
thought she would make a good head girl. The Head Mistress,
however, did not want a Jewish name on the school roll of honour.
Shirley's father, rightly furious, removed her from the school before

Shirley Porter

she was 16 and sent her to Finishing School in Switzerland.

In 1949, aged only 18, she married Leslie Porter, the son of an East End clothing manufacturer. She says: 'I thought he was charming and had lovely blue eyes. He looks a bit like Paul Newman; women still swoon.' Shirley often had a similar effect on the opposite sex, but on account of her tongue rather than her eyes – grown men fainted when confronted with her anger or remorseless demands.

At 22 she was the mother of two children. When they fled the nest she wanted more from life than the routine of well-heeled suburban wife and redundant mother. Not that she was idle. Far from it. She excelled at and took control of everything she touched. She didn't just play golf, she captained and represented the County. She not only helped charities, but Chaired them. She was already a JP when politics beckoned. Elected to Westminster City Council at the age of 43, she was soon manically engaged in battling against the one obsession of her life – Litter.

Paradoxically, ultra right-wing Shirley became a national political figure because of militant left-wing trade unions. For her the Winter of Discontent of 1979 was a stroke of immense good fortune. Government was paralysed by strikes, the dead went unburied and the whole nation became horribly aware of how much waste it produced. Densely populated Westminster suffered badly as its refuse disposal officers went on strike. Adopting the Tesco maxim of 'pile it high', Leicester Square and other public places disappeared beneath a mountain of rotting garbage in black plastic bin liners.

Every bit as revolutionary as her socialist enemies, Shirley proposed to camp out in the Square amongst the refuse as a protest. Smooth as broken glass, she determined to shake the Council out of its polite, non-confrontational, civil-service style. She went out and about in a black mini with blacked-out windows, spying on litter and rubbish; looking, noting and demanding action.

She had a habit, disconcerting for her employees, of walking around 'her' Borough, barking instructions for action into a hand-held tape-recorder. A hapless official would then be ordered to 'Repair by the end of the day and tell me when it is done'. She would sometimes walk home by the same route to check up. A fellow Councillor said admiringly; 'She wore us out. She galvanised people into action. She did a magnificent job with the streets.'

But she did not understand people. 'She had never had the grind of an ordinary job.' She reduced senior executives to tears, ringing them at odd hours of the day and night. She simply did not understand that most people were not consumed with her passion and did not wish to work a 24 hour day. A former Councillor said 'she set impossible deadlines and wanted to test people to destruction'.

Her enthusiasm for brash self-publicity was frowned on by the great and the good of the Tory Party but it worked. It was the age of the Greater London Council, lorded over by Ken Livingstone. Shirley was the only Tory who could match him in the publicity stakes. Styling herself the Westminster Whirlwind she forced the media to pay attention. She personally inaugurated the first Superloo in Westminster, with the press massed in attendance; she did public calisthenics in Hyde Park and, during her manic anti-litter campaign, she both dressed as an Indian squaw and took a camel through the streets to Downing Street.

She was a devotee of the appalling American custom of Power Breakfasts, frequently holding them at her magnificent flat overlooking Hyde Park. These gruesome rituals are ideal symbols to demonstrate that one is far too busy during the rest of the day. The breakfasts were not peaceful affairs. Many of her Council officers, with old-fashioned civil service mind-sets, were laid flat by them and by the terrifying brusqueness of Shirley's demands so early in the morning.

Her taste was just as hectic as the breakfasts. One brow-beaten official described her flat as 'akin to the lighting department at Selfridges' and 'full of appalling cuddly gonks and other soft toys'.

Officers expecting to tuck into a traditional English breakfast were sadly disappointed. Shirley's idea was to eat THEM for breakfast. In any case, no one got any food from the large revolving dumb waiter in the middle of the table – everyone was too busy scribbling and wrestling with paperwork to find answers to the barrage of questions she shot at them.

She hit the headlines in a massive way in the 1980s when she sold three council cemeteries to property speculators for 15p, yes, 15p. They were subsequently re-sold by the speculators for £1.2m. The Council was forced into the ultimate humiliation of having to buy them back.

The revolving doors at WCC spun like a top, spewing out Chief Officers at a rate of about two a year. Worn out by the frenzy, they sought refuge from Westminster's white-water rapids in some more peaceful local government lagoon, undisturbed by exhilarating currents. Anywhere, in fact, to get away from Shirley.

Even the memory of her can send a shiver through former employees, as they re-live the experience of her reign. 'She couldn't help going over the top. She always hogged the conversation at dinner parties unless outranked by a Cabinet Minister, some (but not all) of whom had the ability to get her to shut up.'

'Dominating and difficult to work with, she has a relentlessly sharp tongue.' Margaret Thatcher was an idol and role model. But, even with this most sacred of exemplars, she could not resist the tart observation that, whilst they both had grocers for fathers, 'hers was only a corner shop'.

Strengthened by the invincible certainty that she was right, it followed axiomatically that it was in everyone's interests to have her views and style imposed on them. 'She was capable of making the stiffest of municipal lips quiver with emotion.' Tears were, apparently, commonplace on the eighth floor of Westminster City Hall from whence Dame Shirley presided over the Tory flagship Borough in the 1980s, frequently turning up at the Town Hall looking like a bunny in a pink track suit.

She has been vilified by weaker men (most men are weaker than Dame Shirley). Her enemies deride her sex, her class, her money (she is reputed to be worth around £50m and is ranked the 20th richest woman in the country) and, nastiest of all, her race and religion.

In 1986 the Tories seemed likely to lose control of Westminster. She famously warned in a document circulated to the Conservative group 'Imagine socialists running Buckingham Palace, Militants lording it over Parliament and controlling Downing Street, left-wing extremists interfering in the daily running of business. A horrible nightmare. It certainly is but it could happen to the City of Westminster.' She began to blame people for failing, and bawled them out when they did not have the power and authority to succeed.

She resigned the leadership of Westminster in 1991, was made a Dame and Lord Mayor. Since the glory days life has been tough. She has known personal tragedy. Her only grandson (and heir to the Tesco fortune) was killed, her daughter underwent an acrimonious divorce, her flat in Hyde Park caught fire and some of her business interests foundered.

Politically she never recovered from the 'Homes for Votes' furore in 1994, when leading Westminster councillors were accused of selling council houses with a view to boosting the Conservative vote in marginal wards. The ludicrous use of the name Mr G. Mander on some documents did not help her cause. The scandal forced her to turn her back on her beloved city (she says 'they turned their back on me'). She retreated to Palm Springs, where her energy pulsated unabated – a regular personal trainer, business ventures, plans for a book, speedwalking, t'ai chi and goodness knows what else.

At the time of writing she is battling away in court, fiercely defending herself against the judgment of the auditor whose report criticised her. She may be down but she is far from out for the count – just as one might expect of this icon of the Thatcher years, who was able to hold her own with the Supreme Battleaxe – Margaret Thatcher herself.

Joan Collins OBE

*'I'm tough and I'm strong. And I'm in the right. And I'm not going
to give them their money back.'*

*****

Joan Collins is NOT 'The Bitch'. You'd better believe it. Or she will
chew you into small pieces, spit you out and stamp on you. Then
she'll sue the pants off you. That's official.

Just to be on the safe side then – I believe her. She is definitely not
the celluloid caricature she so often plays. She has spent an
inordinate part of her career playing Battlebitches. As Peregrine
Worsthorne observed, 'Why does someone who, in private, seems
so pre-eminently not a bitch, go to such lengths to give the opposite
impression in her professional life?'

The answer to that is simple. Miss Collins is fond of quoting
Sophie Tucker, 'From birth to 18 a girl needs good parents. From 18
to 25 she needs good looks. From 25 to 50 she needs a good
personality and – from 50 onwards a girl needs good cash.'
Battlebitches like Joan earn good cash.

She certainly looks the part. Pouting lips, bedroom eyes, come-
hither voice, veins 'positively coursing with high-octane
pheromones'. She has been a Star for so long now that, surely, birth
must have been but her first première. Did she emerge in a lighting-
storm of flashbulbs and slink down a catwalk, ready-clad in sling-
back 5" stilettos, 'go-to-hell red' lipstick and shoulder pads built
like barbicans?

Joan Collins

The image of man-eating tigress was perfected in her films *The Stud* and *The Bitch*, both written by little sister Jackie. But the role which established her Battleaxe image was as the wicked, witty, acerbic, archetypal bitch, Alexis Carrington, in *Dynasty* (pronounced, appropriately, 'die-nasty'). With pneumatic cleavage and shoulder pads, she toyed with men and stubbed them out like discarded cigarette ends, using her perfectly arched eyebrows to dispatch them with dramatic effect.

Signed up for one series only, her arrival made *Dynasty* soar up from 35th to 7th in the ratings. So she stayed for nine years and was voted 'Sexiest Bitch on American TV' in 1986. She drove a sexy white Rolls-Royce which, to avoid misunderstandings, sported the number plate '2ND CAR'.

Understandably content with her looks, she says that 'if you don't feel happy witl yourself by the time you are 60 you might as well chuck yourself in the Thames'. Father Time treads warily in her direction, no doubt fearing Alexis' ire if there were even a hint of ageing. Joan posed for *Playboy* when nearly 50 and was voted 'Bird of the Year' by *Sun* readers – ahead of Brigitte Bardot and Raquel Welch. At 65 years old her credo is 'Age is irrelevant – unless you are an antique or a bottle of wine.'

Joan Henrietta Collins was born in Bayswater in May 1933, the daughter of a Romanian-Jewish theatrical agent (once a partner of Lew Grade). Her mother was a blue-eyed blonde, an English Rose. Joan was so stunning that her mother pinned a notice to the pram which read, 'Please do not kiss the baby.'

However, her father described her in less flattering terms declaring 'she looks like half a pound of scrag end'. The agent's critical notice seems less plausible than the producer's. Her father was never a believer in encouragement by flattery. Later, when Joan was voted 'The Most Beautiful Girl in Films' by the Photographers' Association of Britain, he was asked for a comment. 'I am extremely surprised,' he said. He had tried to put her off the world of acting; 'They are vulgar, common and coarse and if that's the profession you want to take up, you'll become just like them.'

Despite this Joan was determined and went to RADA at 15, looking like 'a poor man's Elizabeth Taylor', tried to emulate her and Vivien Leigh. Her first role, in *Lady Godiva Rides Again*, was way down the bill but she already had ambitions to appear in the title role, naked astride the horse.

She thought she wanted to be a stage actress but Hollywood and the J. Arthur Rank School for Young Starlets easily eclipsed the idea of several years of provincial rep in Sheffield or Southend. She was signed up by Rank at the age of 17.

From the age of 19 she combined making bad films with bad marriages. Thereafter, battling and axing husbands became a feature of life. Her approach was practical: 'We owe it to ourselves to be as happy as we can. So, if one is unhappy about being married to someone it is best to get out.' Very Alexis.

By 1987 she had tied the knot four times to husbands described by one commentator as, in chronological order: 'a sadist, a neurotic, a drug user, and a cad.' A lifetime's experience has taught her 'There is a time to get married and a time not to' (mostly not). She now rules out 'absolutely' marriage again for herself, which might seem a little rash when she is only 64 going on 39.

But the record speaks for itself. Her first husband, Maxwell Reed, spiked her drink and took her virginity. She was 17. He was nearly twice her age. The marriage lasted seven months and collapsed when Reed offered to sell her to an Arab sheikh for $10,000. Years later, and fallen on hard times, Reed tried to blackmail her over some photos he had taken of her in the nude.

That was bad enough. But her most disastrous liaison was her fourth marriage, to an unemployed Swedish actor cum double-glazing salesman cum toyboy, Peter Holm. The marriage went down in flames after only six months, surrounded by an acrimonious scrap over (Joan's) money and possessions. Holm showed a commendable attention to detail, listing amongst the chattels he claimed 'the ironing board, chainsaw and assorted screws'.

She takes in her stride bad films, bad mouths, bad marriages and bad men. As well as husbands, she has also had a string of handsome macho lovers. When the inevitable bust-up comes, she can be a shrinking violet, but it's the man who shrinks before the onslaught. One Hollywood second ranker screamed at her on his way out, 'You are a f . . . .. bore.' 'And you are a boring f . . . ' was the instantaneous razor-slash retort.

One of her admirers gave her a stunning and very valuable necklace. The denouement loomed and, naturally enough, Joan wanted to keep the goodies. Why not? They were freely given and she had earned them. On the occasion they parted she was wearing the necklace as they drove across a bridge in New York. Demanding the car be stopped, she got out and, with a dramatic sweep of her perfectly manicured hand, threw the necklace into the river to signify the end of the relationship. What the horrified about-to-be-ex lover did not know was that, sensing things were coming to an end, she had had a copy made and the original remained in her collection.

She avoids lines on the skin but not off the tongue. An elderly innocent, introduced to her at a Hampstead party, recognised neither her face nor her name. Groping for small talk, he asked politely: 'And what do you do?' She flashed a smile: 'Darling, I don't do anything. I just *am*.' More recently an interviewer ventured to suggest she might be tired of being Joan Collins. 'I never, *ever*, ever think that I've got to *be* Joan Collins. I don't know what that means. I *am* Joan Collins.'

Intellectual snobs may look down on her performances and it is true that her 60 films have included the odd critical dubiety. In *Empire of the Ants* she had to crawl around in a Florida swamp and be ravished by giant plastic insects. In *Land of the Pharaohs* (a film which was so bad that it was disowned by its director, Howard Marks) she was caked in Egyptian body make-up and had a giant ruby planted in her navel.

Joan is candid. 'I haven't done *Medea* at the Almeida. But on the other hand, I've never liked that play anyway and the theatre's very small.' So much for Greek tragedy! Actually, after her experiences in *Dynasty*, Medea would be just up Joan's street.

Medea was the Alexis of ancient Greece. She murdered her three sons and killed the mistress of her husband, Jason, by giving her a golden coat impregnated with a poison which caused her to die a horrible, excruciating death after putting it on. Following this happy scene, Jason committed suicide by falling on his sword, having witnessed Medea's escape, gliding through the air in a golden chariot drawn by dragons!

Joan can be similarly determined, if not so literally murderous, when crossed. In 1993, outraged by the invasion of her privacy when America's *Globe* magazine published sneak topless shots of her, snatched as she changed at her Provençal villa, Destino, she sued them and was awarded $1 million damages.

But her revenge on US publisher Random House was even more piquant. The huge American conglomerate gave her a $4 million advance for two books but later sued for its money back, claiming that the novels, *A Ruling Passion* and *Hell Hath No Fury*, were 'primitive, dull, flawed, inane, fragmented, gibberish, clichéd, dated and jumbled.' If that was true, what on earth was the company complaining about? The books obviously had all the essential ingredients of a 'sex and shopping' blockbuster and she had clearly fulfilled her part of the contract.

Stoutly defending herself, Joan said even if the books were unreadable rubbish (which she denied), that was irrelevant. The advance had been paid for the novels regardless of their literary quality. 'They knew I wasn't Hemingway when they signed me.' Quite.

Random House's trial lawyer was despatched by a mixture of alluring looks, husky voice and sympathy-inducing tears. Joan's performance would have won an Oscar for Best Female Actress in a Starring Role, but the lines were her own and she was not acting.

Earlier, outside the court, she was asked how she would repay the company if she lost. In best superbitch manner she replied, 'Oh, darling. I'll just sell a bracelet or something.' But there was no thought of the possibilities of defeat: 'I was threatened. But I'm tough and I'm strong. And I'm in the right. And I'm not going to give them the money back!'

The jury needed little persuasion. Random House were left with a bill described by Miss Collins' lawyers as 'north of £1.3 million'. 'Never,' said Joan, 'had anything tasted so wonderful as the first glass of champagne later that night.'

Described by one commentator as a 'faintly preposterous but

strangely admirable icon of our times', she says she is: 'never judgemental about how other people dress. If Michelle Pfeiffer and Jodie Foster want to go around in a sack then that is for them to decide.'

She flits around the world like a delicate butterfly. 'Travel is my greatest extravagance'. She does it 'the old fashioned way' with up to 47 pieces of luggage – apparently more than Elizabeth Taylor and slightly fewer than Elton John. Travel has its tribulations. She caused a fuss in 1987 when she called a British Airways supervisor a 'f . . . .. old cow' for forcing her to slum it in Club Class when she arrived too late to claim her First Class Seat.

She has experienced several metaphorical earthquakes in her personal life, but wisely sold her Los Angeles home a matter of weeks before the huge literal earthquake. She now says, 'I like to live in a place where I know the earth is not going to move . . . except in the bedroom.'

Recognising a kindred spirit, Joan is a staunch admirer of The Supreme Battleaxe, Lady Thatcher. 'I loved that woman. Loved her.' She is however, less admiring of both the current PM and the Leader of the Opposition. She told an interviewer: 'I mean, take Mr Blair. Call me Tony indeed! Much too blokeish. He's the Prime Minister for heaven's sake. As for Gordon Brown wearing a lounge suit to a black tie dinner . . . That's just downright disrespectful. Whatever next? The Queen opening Parliament in a headscarf and trainers?' William Hague was quickly dismissed: 'Oh darling, he looks like a foetus.'

Has she succeeded by perfecting her bitch roles in real life off-stage? No. Joan decries method acting: 'I think one should immerse oneself in the part on stage but I don't think one should take it home. Do you know the wonderful story about Dustin Hoffman and Laurence Olivier when they were doing *Marathon Man*? Dustin, who is the complete American method actor, said to Olivier, "I just can't feel it today. I just don't feel I can become this character. What am I going to do?" And Olivier said, "Why don't you try acting, dear boy!"'

Playing the part of a Superbitch doesn't exclude a sense of humour. Joan has already chosen her epitaph: 'She had her cake and ate it too.' There is more to life than acting but she is not retiring yet. Joan is indomitable. 'My belief in myself transcends all negativity. Life is a soap opera – and a bowl of cherries.'

Happy and secure in her current long-standing relationship with old Etonian art-dealer Robin Hurlstone (some years her junior, of course), Joan has added more than most to what Dr Johnson called 'the gaiety of nations and the public stock of harmless pleasure'. Given the OBE in 1997, she suggests it was, 'For surviving in a desperately precarious profession for 40 years. I'm The Survivor.'

Elizabeth I
(b.1533 – d.1603)

'I know I have the body of a weak and feeble woman; but I have the heart and stomach of a king, and a King of England too.'
*****

Elizabeth I was one of the greatest English monarchs. 'Gloriana,' 'The Faerie Queene,' the Margaret Thatcher of the sixteenth century! Although women did not get the vote until 1918 Elizabeth dominated the kingdom for nearly half a century from 1558-1603. By force of personality, her shrewd judgement and capacity to inspire loyalty in her subjects, she reigned supreme and successfully.

She had to be a Battleaxe to survive at all in such an era. Her life might easily have ended literally under the axe and her childhood was terrifying. Born in 1533, the political and religious intrigues swirling around the Tudor Court obliged her to grow up at an alarming rate.

'Family values' meant something quite different in Tudor times. Henry VIII divorced two wives and beheaded two others in his desperate search for a male heir to secure the dynasty. Life for his consort became even more precarious than that of the manager of a failing football team today.

Elizabeth was less than three years old when her father beheaded her mother, Anne Boleyn. Even at such a tender age, the child was old enough to appreciate that this awful event had political consequences for her. To regularise affairs Henry had had his marriage to Anne Boleyn annulled on grounds of her previous relationship with Lord Henry Percy. In consequence Elizabeth became illegitimate. Subtly recognising with a sharp but infant intelligence that there had been a change in her status, Elizabeth asked, 'Why Governor, how hap it yesterday Lady Princess and today but Lady Elizabeth?'

Life was no more secure after Henry's demise. He was succeeded by the male heir he had craved. However, Edward VI was only nine years old in 1547 and too young to govern. Affairs of State were superintended by his uncle, Lord Protector Somerset. Within two years Elizabeth narrowly missed being implicated in a treasonous plot to overthrow Somerset's government.

The plotter was actually Thomas, Lord Seymour of Sudeley – who was the Lord Protector's younger brother and, thus, another uncle of Edward's. In a further complication Seymour had secretly married Edward's stepmother, Henry VIII's last wife and widow, Catherine Parr, in whose house Elizabeth continued to live. Seymour was later accused, in addition to treason, of plotting to marry Elizabeth, who was his wife's stepdaughter.

The Tudor game of Happy Families was very confusing indeed. Catherine was Elizabeth's fourth stepmother and she had herself been widowed three times by the age of 35, marrying her fourth husband Seymour (to whom she had been engaged before she caught the king's fancy), within 30 days of Henry's death!

Protector Somerset suspected Elizabeth might have been Seymour's accomplice in an attempt to seize the throne. He sent his brother to the block but Elizabeth, not yet sixteen, escaped by dint of handling herself under interrogation with extreme circumspection. In those days, being in charge was almost as dangerous as being subordinate – Protector Somerset, the subject of his brother's treason, had his own head chopped off for treason shortly afterwards.

After only six years on the throne, her sickly half-brother Edward expired in 1553 – poisoned by the medicines administered to cure him. William Cecil, one of the Secretaries of State, on being told what the doctors were doing to their royal patient, wrote with feeling to another sick friend, 'God deliver you from the physicians.'

Edward was succeeded by his half-sister, Mary, a devout Roman Catholic. Elizabeth then began to suffer an even more terrifying ordeal at the hands of her sister. Aged only twenty she was locked up in the Tower of London. Attempts were made in 1554 to prove her complicity in Sir Thomas Wyatt's rebellion against Mary's marriage to the Catholic fanatic, Philip II of Spain. As next-in-line to the throne and a life-long Protestant, suspicion fell naturally upon Elizabeth. Once again she was saved by the extreme care with which she responded to inquiries, giving 'answerless answers' in the manner of the perfect Permanent Secretary of the 1990s.

In 1558, after a reign of only five years, Mary died. Elizabeth inherited a nation threatened by the danger of internal divisions of religion and external attacks from France and Spain. After the convulsions of the previous twenty years it required exceptional leadership qualities and strength of purpose to overcome them all.

Imposing in appearance, she stood erect with red-gold hair crowning her pale and aquiline features. In spite of possessing the 'manly' attributes essential in a regal Battleaxe, she did not compromise her femininity. In particular she devoted great attention to the maintenance of her looks. Her ladies of the bedchamber attended daily to brush her hair and wash it with alkalised water.

She increasingly applied cosmetics – lotions of white of egg, alum, borax, poppy seeds and powdered eggshell to maintain the whiteness of the skin. To maintain the whiteness of the teeth she used a mixture of white wine and vinegar boiled with honey. These products were all relatively harmless, whereas many pasted their faces with white lead and washed their teeth in aqua fortis, which wrecked the skin and rotted the teeth.

She had an immense wardrobe – in one year alone, 1599, more than £700 was spent on 'fine linen for Her Majesty's person'. An inventory made at about the same time noted 102 'French gownes', 100 'loose gownes' and 67 'round gownes', 99 robes, 127 cloaks, 85 doublets, 125 petticoats, 56 'saufeguardes' (outer skirts), 126 kirtles,

188 'lappe mantles' and 136 'forepartes' (stomachers).

Courtiers had to mind their dress and were forbidden to wear clothes which indicated a higher rank than that to which they could lay claim. It was even more forbidden to wear anything which might be in danger of outshining the Queen herself. Lady Mary Howard presented herself one day in a fabulous dress of velvet and pearls which clearly caught the Queen's envious eye, not to mention the lascivious eye of the Earl of Essex. Asking to borrow the dress (how could Lady Mary refuse?) she put it on but was too tall for it. 'Is it not too short?' she asked Lady Mary, who could only agree. 'Why then,' said the Queen, 'if it become me not as being too short, I am minded it shall never become thee as being too fine. So it fitteth neither well.' Lady Mary could never again wear the dress in the Queen's presence.

Display was essential to the dignity of an absolute monarch but Elizabeth believed also in Thatcherite frugality. As Cecil said 'the parsimony of her Majesty hath been a great cause of her Majesty's riches'. The general costs of her household were £1000 a week by her death. The kitchens consumed well over 20,000 sheep and lambs, 600,000 gallons of beer and 4 million eggs annually. Elizabeth took a close interest in the management of the Exchequer and her own estates, curbing extravagance and waste wherever possible.

She was energetic and loved riding, dancing and rapid walking. Her education was wide – she spoke French, Spanish, Italian, Flemish and Latin. But her greatest attribute was her ability to choose wise and talented advisers like William Cecil, Lord Burghley. Even so she was not easy to work for.

One foreign envoy wrote that she was bossy 'as a peasant upon whom a barony has been conferred'. Even after many years of loyal service she could still imperiously threaten Burghley, 'I have been strong enough to lift you out of this dirt and I am still able to cast you down again.' The Queen was mercurial, mixing such harshness with solicitude, such as when Burghley was suffering from one of his recurrent attacks of gout, 'My lord, we make use of you, not for your bad legs, but your good head.'

Elizabeth, in contrast to her sister 'Bloody' Mary, saw that the divisions in the nation could be contained by tolerance. Though officially establishing the Protestant faith, she permitted private observance of Catholic forms of worship. But, if matters of conscience posed a threat to her government and the stability of the State, she reacted as ferociously as Henry VIII would have done before her.

The Duc de Biron, a troublesome subject of the French King, came on an Embassy with a retinue of over 400 of the leading French families. Elizabeth took him by the hand to London Bridge, gestured upwards to over 300 heads impaled on pikes and said pointedly, 'It is thus we punish traitors in England.'

She was equally ferocious in defending her realm from foreign attack. Following peace overtures from Spain, Elizabeth told the French ambassador, 'The King of Spain is making daily offers of peace and friendship, but I shall not listen to them, knowing his ambition; on the contrary, I have sent Drake to ravage his coasts and am considering sending the Earl of Leycester to Holland to show I am not afraid of war.'

Often assured by her enemies that they had no intention of attacking her, she was not to be taken in. She told the French Ambassador, de Noailles, 'It may be so; but I find it well to be prepared. In times of danger it is the custom of England to arm. If we are well prepared you will be less tempted to meddle with us.'

Although her father had put her mother to death she was proud of her descent from a strong King: 'Although I may not be a lioness, I am a lion's cub and inherit many of his qualities.'

Pope Sixtus V confirmed Elizabeth's view of herself following the execution of Mary Queen of Scots: 'What a valiant woman. She braves the greatest kings by land and sea . . . It is a pity that Elizabeth and I cannot marry: our children would have ruled the whole world.'

When Mary Queen of Scots was scheming to supplant her, Elizabeth declaimed dismissively to the Archbishop of St Andrews, 'I am more afraid of making a fault in my Latin than of the Kings of Spain, France, Scotland, the whole House of Guise and all of their confederates.'

As befits a Battleaxe, she was not only fearless herself but capable of inspiring her troops to instil fear into the enemy. In 1588 England was threatened by the Spanish armada and an invasion army, commanded by the Duke of Parma, massed in the Spanish Netherlands. At Tilbury she made a speech to her troops to rank with the St Crispin's Day speech of Henry V.

'My loving people, We have been persuaded by some that are careful of our safety, to take heed how we commit ourselves to armed multitudes for fear of treachery; but I assure you I do not desire to live in distrust of my faithful and loving people.

'Let tyrants fear. I have always so behaved myself that under God I have placed my chiefest strength and good will in the loyal hearts and good will of my subjects; and therefore I am come amongst you at this time not for my recreation and disport but being resolved, in the midst and heat of the battle, to live or die amongst you all; to lay for God, my kingdom, and for my people, my honour and my blood, even in the dust.

'I know I have the body of a weak and feeble woman; but I have the heart and stomach of a king, and a King of England too, and think it foul scorn that Parma or Spain or any Prince of Europe, should dare to invade the borders of my realm; to which rather than any dishonour should grow by me I myself will take up arms, I myself will be General, Judge and Rewarder of everyone of your virtues in the field.'

She was exceptionally highly-strung, a characteristic sometimes exacerbated by physical pain. She was not a good patient. Complaining of the appearance of a 'desperate ache' in her right thumb, it was diagnosed as 'gout'. But she would not have it. 'The gout it cannot be nor dare it be.'

She was regularly confronted with toothache and was equally obstinate with the dentist. On one occasion the pain was so intense that an extraction was necessary – but no one would dare tell her so because 'she herself doth not or will not think so'. The matter was discussed by the Privy Council, who consulted a tooth-drawer. He advised that the tooth must come out unless dressed with a poultice of fenugreek, which might cause all the neighbouring teeth to fall out. A deputation of Privy Councillors was appointed to deliver the unwelcome news to the Queen. She would not have it – until the

Bishop of London allowed one of his own perfectly healthy teeth to be drawn to demonstrate the ease of the operation!

The Queen was naturally impatient and suffered frequent and extreme bad tempers. 'When she smiles it was a pure sunshine that everyone did choose to bask in if they could, but anon came a storm from a sudden gathering of clouds and the thunder fell in wondrous manner on all alike' wrote Sir John Harington. She would not scruple to slap the face or throw a slipper at the head of some senior courtier or adviser if displeased.

Her mercurial tempers mirrored a deeper inherent irresolution. She often refused to make up her mind on a problem, hoping that events would solve it naturally. Rather than make a decision she would spend weeks in argument and rumination, the endless repetitions driving her ministers to distraction.

Sir Thomas Smith protested, 'It maketh me weary of life. I neither can get the other letters signed, nor the letter already signed permitted to be sent away, but day by day by hour until anon, none, and tomorrow.' Such delays and inconstancies were attributed to having to deal with a woman. One courtier complained, 'This fiddling woman troubles me out of measure. God's wounds! This it is to serve a base, bastard, pissing kitchen woman! If I had served any prince in Christendom, I had not been so dealt withal.'

Her prevarication manifested itself, surprisingly, even in the case of Mary Queen of Scots. Mary's active complicity in the Babington plot of 1586, which had compassed the murder of Elizabeth, resulted in her condemnation to death. But Elizabeth was loth that the sentence should be carried out. She postponed the sitting of Parliament several times because she knew that both Houses would urge her to sign Mary's death warrant. It took the Government three months of increasing pressure to secure her consent. When Mary was beheaded, Elizabeth threw an hysterical fit and declared that she had never authorised or intended that the deed should be done.

Her reluctance owed nothing to any humanitarian or merciful impulse. It was only because of Mary's royal blood and the regicide example which such an execution would set that she stayed her hand. She knew also that execution would lead to great diplomatic problems even amounting to war with France and Spain.

The non-royal conspirators, however, bore the full brunt of her merciless wrath. In a fury of resentment she exclaimed that hanging was too good for them and she wrote to Burghley the day before their trial to urge him to tell the judge to deliver the usual sentence of death but, 'for more terror' to remit the manner of execution to the Queen and her Council.

Burghley objected that the existing penalty was quite horrible enough – in fact was so cruel that it was normally seen to that the victim was dead before disembowelling and emasculation took place. If this sentence were carried out to the letter in the sight of the people it would serve perfectly well to deter future attempts at assassination. But Elizabeth was not satisfied.

In the case of the treasonous commoners the executioner was obedient to the Queen's wishes 'to protract the extremity of their pains in the sight of the multitude'. They were still alive when they were taken down from the gallows, and when he took his knife and began to cut open their stomachs and pull out the entrails in front of their faces. It was a scene of such bloodthirsty butchery, which caused such an uproar of disgust amongst the crowd, that Elizabeth was implored to give orders to ensure that the next batch of prisoners should be dead before the drawing and quartering began. Reluctantly, she was prevailed upon to be merciful.

Although she could be implacably brutal, she could also be forgiving when she wished. A lady of Bloody Mary's household had been particularly cruel to Elizabeth during her sister's reign. Upon Elizabeth's accession she asked most abjectly for pardon, and received the following response, 'Fear not, we are of the nature of the lion, and cannot descend to the destruction of mice and such small beasts.'

Edward de Vere, Earl of Oxford, once made a low obeisance to the Queen when he accidentally broke wind. He was so overcome with embarrassment that he felt obliged to exile himself in travel abroad for seven years. When he came home the Queen was all solicitude. Virtually her first words to him were, 'My Lord I had forgot the fart.'

Elizabeth was an undoubted Battleaxe long before the term was coined. Nonetheless she was truly popular in an age of absolutism when popularity mattered not a jot. As the Queen said, in response to a plea from Parliament to marry and settle the succession: 'As for my own part I care not for death; for all men are mortal. And though I be a woman, yet I have as good a courage, answerable to my place, as ever my father had. I am your anointed Queen. I will never be by violence, constrained to do anything. I thank God I am endued with such qualities that if I were turned out of the realm in my petticoat, I were able to live in any place in Christendom.'

Lady Sarah Graham Moon

'If I'd had a gun I would have killed him.'
*****

In May 1992 there was a sudden and total eclipse of the Moon, which came as a complete surprise to astronomers. The eclipse involved not the familiar heavenly body but an earthy baronet – the overblown and adulterous Sir Peter Graham Moon, familiarly known as Hippo and described by his wife, Sarah, as 'a great fat fool'.

Sir Peter's flaunting of a new girlfriend provoked Lady Moon beyond endurance. She then flashed like a meteor through the sky to make her protest. Had she carried out her real feelings (`If I'd had a gun I would have killed him') she would, by now, be languishing at Her Majesty's Pleasure, but a grateful nation was enthralled instead by the delicious details of her infinitely more piquant revenge.

Sarah Moon's father, Lt Colonel Michael Lyndon-Smith, was a doctor with the World Health Organisation when she was born in Poona, the eldest of five. Spending her wartime childhood in Egypt, she went to school at Benenden, followed by the normal social whirl, becoming one of the last debutantes to be presented at Court.

Sir Peter was her second mistake. Her first was to marry, far too young, Major Anthony Chater. She was a 'virtual virgin' on her wedding night which apparently 'terrified her'. She clearly recovered her composure and had three children by him before she

_____ 82 _____

was 24. He then announced he was leaving her and the marriage ended in 'a vicious vitriolic battle' with the Major keeping custody of the children.

It was a case of 'Once bitten, please bite me again.' Little over a year later she married once more – the 'fun loving' Sir Peter, already by then on the way to bankruptcy. Two sons arrived and, although a family trust provided for the children, Lady Moon personally had difficulty making ends meet. Her husband, meanwhile, continued to indulge his passion for expensive tailoring, vintage wines, luxury cars and women.

The new Moon waxes to full Moon but then wanes. The Moon marriage followed the astronomical course – it deteriorated and Lady Moon had 'no more use of her husband in bed'. They had separated in all but name, living at opposite ends of a house in Berkshire with a decree absolute pending.

All might have continued the way of so many British marriages with the husband, or indeed the wife, having affairs on the side, but for the fact that Sir Peter exhibited the grossest bad taste by moving in with his latest girlfriend, Amanda Acheson, near by.

'Doing it under my nose was the final clod of earth in my face. He could at least have gone over the hill.' She didn't want him but no one else was going to have him right on her doorstep.

Lady Moon decided to put a gloss on the story – in fact six litres of white gloss paint. Her revenge began when she strode to the driveway of Amanda's cottage at 3.00 a.m. and solemnly poured it all over Sir Peter's gleaming blue BMW – his pride and joy.

This might have been enough for many women who would have been aghast at the damage they had caused. But not for Lady Moon.

She was further roused to anger some days later when she telephoned the mistress, asking to talk to her husband. Amanda, rubbing salt in the wound, announced she would 'see if I can get him out of bed'. Whilst waiting to see if she could, Lady Moon began to clean out the chicken houses. When Sir Peter had neither returned her call nor arrived in person after the sixth such house she snapped, put a sledgehammer through the windows at his end of the house, and went inside to cut off the sleeves of his thirty-two Savile Row Suits.

This hurt Sir Peter in one of his tenderest spots. His suits, like his cars, were his treasured possessions. When he finally arrived, puffing up the drive, it was just in time to see her dousing boxes of his finest Romeo & Julieta Havana cigars in the animals' drinking trough. For the hapless baronet there was little romance about this story of moon-crossed lovers.

Lady Moon had not waned yet. The Grand Finale, a few days later, was an inspiration to women everywhere. She descended to Sir Peter's cellar, loaded 70 or so bottles of his most valuable vintage claret and port into milk crates, and stowed them in the back of the family Volvo. She sped off to East Garston, site of the new Moon love-nest, with the Château Lafite 1961 clanking around in the boot. Bottles were liberally distributed on the doorsteps of lucky villagers, to be discovered with the morning milk; some were left by the War Memorial and still more generally dotted around the village.

At 6.00 a.m. the local milkman, realising something of what had happened, took pity on Sir Peter. He collected up a crateload of wine and delivered it back to him. However, others could not believe their eyes – and their luck. Amongst the early risers to notice this Manna from the Moon were some lads from the nearby racing stables. They whipped the horses back into their stables, delayed the morning exercise, and lost no time in shovelling up some unexpected liquid winnings – far more palatable than what they were used to shovelling.

Sir Peter fled abroad, married wife No. 2, separated within six months, only to pop up again in the Home Counties in 1998, Thai-ed down by a 19-year-old Thai teenager called Mem, and running a country pub. Lady Moon went on to found the Old Bags' Club for abandoned wives of a certain age. She has admitted to loneliness but retains her sense of humour. She tells how on one occasion she was asked to dinner by a married friend who mused aloud on the telephone as to whom she might invite '. . . for you . . .' 'Don't bother,' said Lady Moon. 'I'll share your old man.' There was a silence at the end of the line while her friend pondered whether a lady who could wreak such stylish revenge on her own husband might just not be joking.

She now calls her actions 'my ghastly atrocities' but thousands of women throughout Britain say, 'Shine on Lady Moon'.

Bessie Braddock

(b.1899 – d. 1970)

'I wish I had a machine gun on the lot of you; you are all rats. We have a corporation rat catcher but he goes for the wrong sort.'
(Addressing Conservatives in Liverpool City Council Chamber)
*****

Bessie was born in 1899. Her parents were trade union activists in Liverpool and Bessie became a militant in her pram. 'It's true,' she said, 'I was a handful. I wanted my own way and played hell if I didn't get it. Mother was tolerant. Even the day I flung the piano stool at Enid, and missed; the stool sailed through the window.'

Aged only 12 she stood with her mother on the platform during a dock strike, rousing the workers into inactivity. In the pre-Mandelson era, propaganda was a less sophisticated art – Bessie put 'Workers of the World Unite' stickers on the rump of cows in Cheshire lanes as she cycled round with her friends. Her parents were fiercely opposed to the First World War and Bessie's real political baptism came as she distributed leaflets at anti-war meetings.

In the Twenties, post-war boom gave way to unemployment and depression. Bessie spoke at meetings for the unemployed, where she met John Braddock, their local organiser. So began a lifelong partnership that would see them constantly in the eye of the political storm in Liverpool. They married when Bessie was 23 and both were communists.

Bessie Braddock

In pre-Stalinist days, true communists rejected marriage as bourgeois. Bessie's romantic excuse for tying the knot was that, if John went to prison again for communist activities, it would make it easier to keep in touch. John was an inveterate inciter of riots and continued to be sent to prison long after leaving the Communist Party. In 1932 he was re-elected to the City Council from Walton Gaol.

A fervent revolutionary, Bessie loved underground cloak and dagger activities which were often criminal. To ease the movement of comrades from overseas she set up a team, conveniently composed of deaf mutes so they could not give themselves away, to provide fake trade union cards and meal tickets. Pockets were picked for the cause, and Bessie had her own network of secret agents to infiltrate rival outfits of both Left and Right. There was even talk of gun running and some kind of 'friendly tie-up' with the IRA. Bessie was well equipped to take care of herself. Always a big girl, she threw her weight behind the cause, learning judo to scatter all in her path. She wrote in her memoirs, 'This was a war in which we acknowledged no rules. We had no respect for the law . . . we never considered fair play.'

Bessie and Jack began to dislike the authoritarian streak in communism and suspected that Nanny Moscow did not necessarily know best for the British working man and woman. They resigned from the Party in 1924, abandoned bloody revolution and turned to more mundane municipal methods. They were both elected to Liverpool City Council, with John rising to become first socialist Leader of the Council.

Bessie, with her formidable frame, was no shrinking violet and brought her street fighter's experience into the Council Chamber. She caused 'the wildest disorder that ever took place', once employing a two-foot-long megaphone to yell at the Conservatives 'I wish I had a machine gun on the lot of you; you are all rats. We have a corporation rat catcher but he goes for the wrong sort.'

Her acerbity embarrassed her more faint-hearted, moderate-minded colleagues. She was often escorted out of the Chamber for refusing to stop arguing when she had been ruled out of order or for refusing to withdraw insulting personal remarks, for example, that a fellow member was 'a deliberate liar' or 'a blasted rat'.

Eventually moving right across the socialist spectrum from Communist to right-wing Labour, she mellowed not one jot. In the Labour landslide of 1945 she became Liverpool's first woman MP. She made her intentions clear in her maiden speech on housing, promising to 'kick up a row'. Her constituents were living in 'bug-ridden, lice-ridden, lousy hell holes' and she demanded action.

With her generous bulk, rosy countenance and bellowing 'scouse' voice she was a fearsome sight in the Commons. She sat in the front seat below the gangway, ample thighs spreading over two seats, glaring ferociously at the wicked Tories opposite. If Parliament had been televised in her day, clips of her would have been restricted to the period after the 9 o'clock watershed, like the films of Vincent Price and Peter Cushing.

She made her presence felt very shortly after she was elected. During a debate on the Transport Bill, she led other Labour Members in a demonstration across the Floor to occupy seats left vacant by absent Conservatives. Mrs Braddock planted her ample frame in the one usually occupied by Winston Churchill. The *Bolton Evening News* reported her manner of crossing the Floor as 'dancing a jig', observing that the 'whole performance was nauseating, a sorry degradation of democratic government'. Bessie sued for libel on the jig allegation. In the absence of television to confirm or deny how she had disported herself, MPs (including both Chief Whips), pressmen and Officers of the House trooped into the witness box to give their account of what happened.

It was alleged that, with her hands on her hips 'she made a few steps forward, a few steps backwards and then arched her body (a somewhat improbable manoeuvre, given her tank-like super-structure!) and minced across the floor'. There was a conflict of evidence, especially as some 18 months had passed since the alleged incident, but it took the jury only 40 minutes to find for the newspaper.

It was an exciting time to be in the House of Commons and Bessie was always in the scrum. 'Chips' Channon recorded in his diary one of many kerfuffles on the morrow of the Socialist triumph of 1945:

'First class row last night. Strachey making very bad speech. Lindsay called him fascist. Socialists infuriated. Hogg lost his temper. Strachey's words drowned in hubbub. Nearly some free fights. Mrs Manning wanted to hit Hinchinbrooke. Chief Whip had to push Lindsay out of way. Baxter thought he was being manhandled and a socialist hit him in the face. Waldron Smithers tried to push into the middle of the scrum and shoved Lady Davidson out of the way. She turned on him. He told her to shut her b— mouth. Eddie Winterton was delighted and said it was like old times when the Irish nationalists were still there. Mrs Braddock sat on the sidelines and kept chanting 'Hooligans. Hooligans. Hooligans.'

Bessie was a fearless champion of the poor and the oppressed. Unable to detect any saving grace in any Conservative, she hated 'Toryism, capitalism and the boss-class'. Nevertheless she became the hammer of the Left in her own Party, passionately opposing Aneurin Bevan, the leader of the Left in Labour's bitter internal conflicts of the 1950s. Many were perplexed at this as she seemed such a natural radical and rebel herself. She feared, however, that they were too close to the communists, whom she had so comprehensively rejected.

Jack had been an amateur boxer and Bessie was an ardent supporter of boxing as 'an opportunity to let off steam in controlled circumstances'. She was 'Very Old Labour' and Honorary President of the Professional Boxers' Association. Her bouts with the middle-class Dr Edith Summerskill, who thought boxing was degrading and brutalising and tried to ban it, were legendary. Colleagues fought for a ringside seat. In 1953 she received a medal 'For Services to Boxing' presented in the ring at the Liverpool Stadium. She was told 'You have done more for British boxing than two heavyweights.'

She faced hecklers, and indeed the world, four-square with chin jutting out. Heckled by the Left at a London Labour Party rally in Hyde Park she countered, 'I'm not afraid of any of you. When you reach the stage where you are unable to control yourself you are no use to the Labour movement at all.'

At election time her canvassing was unconventional. She merely strode down each street shouting 'Come out and vote' adding, if thought necessary for further encouragement, 'We're losing'. A far cry from the subtleties of current spin-doctors but it worked; they voted for her in their droves.

At Westminster she later became Chairman of the Commons Catering Committee and appeared in the Chamber to answer Parliamentary Questions on such vital issues as the 'scandalous rise in the price of custard in the cafeteria from 1d to 3d'. In 1965 the most popular meal in the dining room was still the three-course lunch or dinner at four shillings and sixpence, a price which had remained unchanged since 1956. Swingeing increases had to be made to reduce the ballooning deficit. Members squealed but Bessie saw them off with all the flinty intransigence of a Victorian mill-owner.

She was, incidentally, succeeded by none other than the hon. and gallant Member for Buckingham, Captain Robert Maxwell MC MP. He proposed to deal with the deficit by selling much of the magnificent wine cellar, built up over years, including many rarities which MPs were able to consume at knock-down prices based on historic costs. The wines were valued and the best vintages sold to a willing buyer. It was discovered, conveniently long afterwards, that the sale had considerably underestimated the true market value and the wines had been decanted into the cellars of Headington Hill Hall owned by none other than the said Captain Maxwell himself!

Bessie was renowned as a battling constituency MP, on one occasion bringing an unexpected whiff of Clochemerle to Liverpool. The Council of British Sanitary Pottery Manufacturers complained to her that the fittings in the men's lavatories at Lime Street Station fell short of the standard appropriate to such an important rail terminal, especially one used (in those days of thriving ocean liner traffic) by overseas visitors. Bessie, as local MP, decided to investigate for herself. While she descended the stairs to the men's urinals, a railway police inspector and a sergeant stood guard for 13 minutes until she emerged, flushed but triumphant, to confirm that the facilities were indeed second rate.

She was loved by her constituents, many of whom thought she

could solve all their problems with a wave of her magic wand. One morning, as she was about to leave her office after a packed surgery, she heard someone thundering frantically on the locked door. Although ravenous for lunch, Bessie would never turn anyone away. She unbolted the door to find a young man in wild distress shouting, 'Save Us! Save Us! For God's sake save us!' Quickly pulling him inside, she calmed him down and tried to prise out of him which 999 service to call, only to discover that the miracle he wanted her to perform was to save Liverpool from relegation to the Second Division.

She did once meet her match whilst judging a dog show at Southport. A Dobermann pinscher pinched her velvet hat from her head. Mrs Braddock grabbed the hat, but the dog would not let go. She snarled and tugged; the dog snarled and tugged. There was much to-ing and fro-ing but an impasse occurred until the owner intervened to separate the combatants. Bessie commented, 'I suppose every dog must have its day and it must have been his.'

Bessie never used a trace of make-up in her life and was not a natural on the catwalk, being just 5' 2" tall with a 50 inch bust, 40 inch waist, 50 inch hips and weighing nearly fifteen stone. But, in the cause of outsize women, she gamely tried her hand at modelling on TV to show that stout women could look sleek on slender means. She disported herself in an interesting turquoise rayon crêpe dress, with pleated skirt and matching jacket.

Clothes continued to be rationed for a number of years after the war and Bessie campaigned for extra clothing coupons for outsize ladies. She attacked the unfairness of charging more purchase tax on larger size clothes, which cost more because they used more cloth. A woman with 48" hips ('outsize') had to pay at least 13 shillings more for a dress than her slimmer cousin with 38" hips ('stock size'). Likewise, a blouse up to 38" bust was two-thirds the price of one 40" and over. As one woman in four was 'outsize' at the time, it was a popular cause.

Bessie's behaviour in 1952 during a 23-hour debate on unemployment in the Lancashire textile industry was described as 'not seemly for the House of Commons' and she became the first woman to be suspended following a series of challenges to the authority of the Speaker. Concerned about the future of the Cotton Exchange in her constituency, she had been bobbing up and down like a cork since 1.50 a.m. trying to catch the Speaker's eye. She could contain herself no longer when at 9.30 a.m., after nearly eight hours, the Minister rose to wind up and she had not been called.

Gesticulating wildly, she declared she had been ignored deliberately by the Deputy Speaker, had been promised (as she had) that she would be called and needed to speak before the Minister so he could answer her in his own speech. All perfectly reasonable but the Deputy Speaker was unmoved. Huffing and puffing like a steam engine, she refused to resume her seat declaring, 'I refuse to sit down. I refuse to sit down. I am just not going to sit down' and subsequently refused to withdraw from the Chamber.

The Speaker himself was summoned and Bessie was 'named' (MPs are normally referred to by their constituency except when the Speaker suspends them, when they are referred to by name). If the Member refuses to withdraw, the Speaker instructs the Serjeant at Arms to remove the offender – if necessary at the point of his sword, he being the only person entitled to bear arms in the Chamber. Bessie flounced out of the Chamber, magnanimous in defeat, declaring that she would go 'with pleasure'. Colleagues had urged her to go quietly to spare the embarrassment of the Serjeant at Arms who was 'old and not very strong'. She would have been the immovable object to his rather too resistible force.

On another occasion she asked the Speaker whether she could throw an egg at a doubting Thomas Tory MP who did not believe that the one she was holding in her hand for demonstration purposes was real. Permission was not granted!

During a debate on firearms she produced from her capacious handbag two air-pistols, brandished them above her head and then proceeded to 'fire' them at the Conservative benches. She then broke yet another cardinal rule of the House by crossing the Floor and thumping them down on the Table in front of the Home Secretary.

Never in awe of grandees, and certainly not Conservative ones, she declared of Quintin Hogg (earlier and later Lord Hailsham) that she 'would like to smack his behind for what he says'. She also refused to sign the 80th birthday book tribute to Sir Winston Churchill, objecting to the adulatory words inscribed at the front. 'There was a hell of a row about it but I wouldn't sign his book . . . it would have made me a hypocrite.'

No believer is more zealous than a convert. Despite the fact that her mother had collaborated with Lenin himself in drawing up the statutes of the British Communist Party, Bessie caused considerable upset to the Soviet police on a visit to Russia in 1956. She was highly outspoken, stopping to address crowds on street corners, severely criticising the regime with all the vigour of a Liverpool mob orator. The Mayor of Odessa, her host, was moved to remark 'she is always looking for trouble' – perhaps fearing that when she was safely out of the country he might be even more safely in Siberia.

In the 1950s her implacable opposition to Aneurin Bevan became more and more outspoken and this caused heightened tension with her constituency party. She said openly that Nye had done more to weaken the Labour movement than anyone since the 1930s and once rendered him (unusually) speechless by telling him to his face, 'You're a bloody liar'. She believed strongly in liberty and equality but was not so bothered about fraternity!

Nye (then at the height of his reputation as Minister of Health) told a Conference of Labour women that 'he was not going to be dictated to by a lot of frustrated females'. Bessie, incandescent, barged in and cornered him like a rabbit in his office at the Ministry of Health. She gave him an 'almighty drubbing', so much so that his wife, Jennie Lee, said 'I had never seen him so upset.'

She relented a little in later years, particularly when Bevan himself turned on the Left, but she retained her suspicions and transferred her opposition after his death to his disciple and successor in his Ebbw Vale constituency, Michael Foot, who continued to carry the Left's mantle. They were due to speak together at a Durham Miners' Gala in 1961. The night before there was a terrible storm and Lord Lawson (Labour Secretary of State for War in 1945) was woken by his wife in some concern at the noise. 'Go to sleep,' he told her, 'that's not thunder, that's Bessie getting ready to deal with Michael Foot.'

In 1954 her Left-wing constituency party proposed that she

should retire and not fight the next election. Labour's National Executive Committee held an inquiry and rejected the proposal. The next year the constituency carried a similar motion. Again the NEC overruled it. Much bad blood had been spilled, her constituency officers resigned and an independent Labour candidate stood against her. Bessie swept all majestically before her and was returned with a majority of 7,186.

She finally retired after 24 years because of poor health and the earlier death of her Jack on whom she relied heavily.

Nicola Horlick

'If you're going to succeed in life you need to be determined. If you're not, if you're just a wimp and let people walk all over you, you're never going to get anywhere.'

*****

'Horlicks!' – the word used to be indelibly associated with milky drinks to settle the stomach and induce sleep. But all that changed on 17 January 1997, when it acquired a diametrically opposite meaning.

Nicola Horlick surged through the tabloids, just as she had earlier crashed through the City, like a rhinoceros on heat. Mrs Horlick was in a towering rage. She had just been fired from her high-flying job managing £18 billion of pension fund assets for investment bank, Deutsche Morgan Grenfell – which in 1996 had netted her a 'pay package' of £1.15 million.

'Nicola Horlick is absolutely bloody terrifying.' She displays all the vigour, energy, indomitability and hurricane-force personality of a true Battleaxe. In the course of one week she was both promoted to one of the top positions in DMG and also sacked (or 'suspended' in bankspeak). She responded in the way Battleaxes do. She declared war on her German-owned employer and embarked on a reverse blitzkrieg. After a fruitless whirlwind assault on the London branch she set out on a 'drang nach Osten' to Frankfurt, to confront the Teutonic top brass.

Looking back, Nicola was a born rebel and ran away from

Nicola Horlick

Cheltenham Ladies College when only fourteen. Two kindly policemen found her wandering at the railway station and tried to help. She refused to give them her name and when one tried to look in her bag to ascertain her identity she demanded to know whether he had a search warrant and threatened dire consequences if either dared to lay a finger on her.

She was born hyperactive, needs only six hours sleep a night and 'feels ill' if she indulges in what most normal people regard as the simple luxury of a 'lie-in'. Married with five children (one only seven months old at the time), she said: 'I go back to work for a rest.' Her children were meticulously planned so they arrived precisely when she could combine maternity leave with the Christmas break. When someone ventured to suggest that this vision of 'poor Tim Horlick instructed to remove his pyjamas on a certain date at the appointed time' might just have taken some of the romance away she responded robustly: 'Nonsense. I have a perfect 28-day cycle. I know precisely when I am ovulating.'

Nicola's abilities as a juggler of family and funds excite admiration and respect. But she has her enemies too: 'I think she is an appalling woman!' said one former colleague, who added that she stood out as nakedly ambitious even in the City. 'She has this indomitable sense of her own rightness,' said another.

Yes, she is fiercely ambitious but also spectacularly successful and she inspired devotion from the young tyros in her charge. But, in the game of musical chairs after the sacking of the Chief Executive in September 1996, Horlick was denied the promotion she hoped for. A Battleaxe is used to getting her own way. Dissatisfied with moving only £18 billion out of the £70 billion of assets controlled by DMG, for Nicola the grass began to look greener elsewhere.

Subordinates sniffed the air and realised change might be afoot. Rumours abounded. Annual bonuses might not be as much as expected. The team leader might be off. So the team also got itchy feet which was quite understandable. If you were a 20-something fund manager on a mere £60,000 a year you could be forgiven for feeling underpaid, especially if you feared your bonus for the year would amount to a measly £35-40,000 on top.

Speculation permeated the air like joss sticks. Would a competitor company poach Horlick and her whole team of Young Turks? Would DMG be left with an army of blue-chip clients but no one to service them? Would this lead to a takeover?

In this frenetic atmosphere Horlick was first promoted and, only four days later, sacked – on suspicion of secretly organising a mass exodus of the company's staff to a rival. In the meantime startling scenes were played out in the counting-house.

Our redoubtable heroine, as highly-strung as the red braces of an Essex City boy, ran out of one over-charged meeting in tears and sought refuge in the loo. In a scene of high excitement she then flew from the building. One senior fund manager fell to his knees and started barking like a dog. It was an everyday story of City folk.

The denouement was quite a day. At 7.30 a.m. her husband Tim left their five-storey Kensington home to go to work. A throng of journalists was already standing vigil on the doorstep. Nicola was 'very well, thank you'. No, he had no idea what she was up to for the rest of the day – probably closeted with lawyers. If only he had known!

At 8.00 a.m. the nanny left, taking the three eldest daughters to school. At 8.15 a.m. the pack of humble seekers-after-truth parked outside had hardened themselves to the likelihood of a morning's utter tedium, with nothing to do but talk to other journalists.

Suddenly, the front door swung open and they heard, like the opening bars of the Prelude to Act 3 of Wagner's *Lohengrin*, the chromatic yet commanding tones of Mrs Horlick: 'I am going to feed my baby and then we are going to the offices of Morgan Grenfell. You will all be coming with me.'

In authoritative tones which brooked no argument she boomed, 'I am going to ask Robert Smith to reinstate me. The legal process takes too long. I'm going to have to take matters into my own hands.

'I believe in the truth. I insist that people listen to me. And I WILL be heard!' With that clarion call, mother swept back inside – youngest daughter strapped to her like the figurehead under the bowsprit of a three-decker man o'war.

At 8.36 a.m. precisely Nicola burst forth again in a Morticia

Addams-style black suit, whose severity was leavened only by a long single string of pearls. Another overture of justification. And then: 'It is utterly disgraceful. Justice should be done.' With barely a pause for breath, she ordered: 'Now! I shall meet you at Finsbury Circus. By the office.'

With that she poured herself into her red Alfa Romeo sports car and, turbo-charged with passion, swept off in a cloud of dust towards the City.

At 9.10 a.m. she had reached the enemy front-line. Like Evelyn Waugh's Mrs Stitch she mounted the pavement to avoid the traffic, parked, checked everyone was all present and correct and swept like a tornado, a pearl-wind, into DMG's London HQ, engulfing and overwhelming the security guards and anyone else who got in the way.

Then began her assault on the building A security guard, primed to repel boarders, stepped forward but quickly stepped back, demoralised and defeated by the fearsome eye contact. 'If you lay a finger on me or these people, I shall call the police. I am just so angry.'

Although not aerodynamically designed for a rapid ascent, she charged up four flights of stairs, the retinue of hacks panting in her wake. On arrival in the holy of holies she cut a swathe through the ranks of young, gaping-mouthed, stripe-shirted desk-wallahs and strode into the office of Robert Smith, Chief Executive of Morgan Grenfell Asset Management.

Alas! The opera did not live up to the overture. He was out! Not to be outdone, she decided there and then to make a frontal assault on the Big Cheese of DMG himself. On to Bishopsgate to confront Chief Executive Michael Dobson. The ratpack dutifully scrambled down the backstairs and into the street.

At 9.45 a.m. she marched into reception at Bishopsgate. 'I wish to see Mr Dobson and, if he will not see me within 20 minutes, you may inform him that I shall be going to Germany.' Understandably alarmed, Dobson had barricaded himself in his bunker and refused to see her. The minutes ticked by. At the expiration of exactly 20 minutes Mrs Horlick was informed that no one was available to see her.

Nicola, contemptuous but undaunted, addressed her troops, the open-mouthed hacks – 'To Germany!' she cried, 'I'm fighting for justice and you will be coming with me.'

It was just like 3 September 1939 all over again. The historians amongst the hacks remembered Chamberlain's mournful broadcast after no reply was received to the British Government's 11 a.m. ultimatum: 'I have to tell you now that no such undertaking has been received and this country is – at war with Germany.'

By 1.00 p.m. Nicola was sipping a glass of sparkling mineral water on the plane for Frankfurt, together with those from the press who had managed to get permission to follow their leader and secure a seat on the plane. At 3.45 p.m. touchdown and a pause to phone the lawyers back in London. A slight technical hitch. Er . . . where were we going? What is Deutsche Bank's address?

'I have never seen these people. And I don't speak German.' A short telephone conversation later and . . . : 'Well, they are not prepared to see me. But I shall go anyway. Come along, follow me.'

A Panzer division of taxis set off in formation, now swelled also by the ranks of the German Press. On to the Deutsche Bank Tower.

By 4.30 p.m. Mrs Horlick had her tanks parked on the manicured lawns of Deutsche Bank. Politely, in spite of the earlier verbal rebuff, she was invited in and upstairs to meet the head of security who told her that someone would see her after all.

The minutes ticked away. At 6.00 p.m. the waiting Press were told Mrs Horlick had already left by the back door and was on her way to the airport. The hacks set off in hot pursuit. It had been a hard, frenetic day with much food for thought but no thought for food. There was just time to grab a small snack of *Lachs gebraten am Stück in Weisswein mit Salat von geräuchertem Aal und Stangenspargel*, swilled down with a refreshing glass of *Iphöfer Domherr Schwarzriesling Weissherbst Kabinett*. Sadly, the names took so long to pronounce that, by the time the food arrived, there was no time left to eat before boarding the plane to Heathrow.

By 10.00 p.m. Mrs Horlick was stepping down on the tarmac, clutching a carrier bag of presents which somehow she had found time to buy for the children. She charged off towards her car and sped off home – where Mr Horlick was waiting, just possibly wondering where she had been all day and, no doubt with a hot milky drink.

In spite of all her inspirational efforts, Nicola did not get her job back. But, she has become an overnight media sensation and that one episode alone would have earned her a place in this book! She did not tarry long on the unemployment register and was soon snapped up by the French bank, Société Générale. She also wrote her own book, *Can You Have It All?*, generously giving the proceeds to Great Ormond Street Children's Hospital which cared for her eldest daughter, Georgie. She concluded that you can't have it all – and if she can't then no one can.

Nancy Astor
(b.1879 – d.1964)

'I haven't anything against men but Eve showed which was the weaker.'
****

'She is not a lady as you would understand a lady,' Nancy Astor's butler informed the new lady's maid, describing her employer-to-be.

According to George Bernard Shaw she was 'a recklessly unladylike lady, a violently Radical conservative, a prohibitionist member of the liquor trade Party and the most turbulent member of the Party of Order.' She was a mass of contradictions, bossy, opinionated, didactic and self-assured to the point of infallibility (in her own opinion at least).

Nancy was married first to a rich Bostonian, Robert Gould Shaw. One of her sons wrote, 'He supposed he was marrying a typical Southern belle . . . but awoke from his reverie with the surprise of a man who had unsuspectingly got into bed with a wild cat.' She divorced him after six years on the grounds of his alcoholism, and sailed for England.

Never one to waste time, she met her second husband, Waldorf Astor, on the boat. 'I came to England to hunt a fox not a husband but I was overpersuaded and married beneath me . . . most women do.' Asked later whether her husband was a millionaire she retorted, 'I certainly hope so. That's one of things I married him for.' She had plenty of money of her own but she used to say 'I didn't marry an Astor to spend my own money.'

She came to love England with the vehemence of a convert whilst main' ⸱ ning her pride in her Virginian ancestry. 'You can't be a snob if you're a Virginian because we can't imagine anyone being above us.' At a dinner hosted by President Theodore Roosevelt Nancy was given precedence over Grace Vanderbilt. To smooth the ruffled feathers Nancy told Mrs Vanderbilt, 'The Astors skinned skunks a hundred years before the Vanderbilts worked ferries.'

Much later, in another expression of democratic spirit and despite being married to a viscount, she proposed the abolition of the hereditary peerage to get rid of snobbery. 'You can have women who in their own right cannot sit in the House of Lords but any old male mumbo-jumbo can sit there.' (Peeresses were not allowed to sit until 1958).

When she encountered English snobbery she repelled it with withering scorn. Mrs Gordon Cunard said to her, 'I suppose you have come over here to get one of our husbands.' Nancy immediately replied, 'If you knew the trouble I've had getting rid of my first, you'd know I don't want yours.'

In 1910 Waldorf was elected MP for Plymouth, but his father died in 1919 and he went to the House of Lords, having succeeded as Viscount Astor. In turn Nancy succeeded Waldorf as MP and became world famous as the first woman to take her seat at Westminster. In recognition of this unique event, she was introduced into the Commons by the former Conservative Prime Minister Arthur Balfour and the then Prime Minister David Lloyd George, a Liberal. She held the seat for 25 years, much of her support coming from women and Liberals. Although elected as a Conservative, she sat wherever her fancy dictated.

For nearly two years she was the only woman MP and held her own with outrageous panache. She refused to become an honorary man and said women were 'not looking for superiority. We've always had that. All we want is equality.' She said of herself, 'I ceased to be a person and became a symbol of the aspirations of women and a champion of their rights. Others might have brought more intellectual weight to the task but she combined femininity, independence of spirit, wit and charm to devastating effect. Waldorf later observed, 'When I married Nancy I hitched my wagon to a star. When she got into the House I found I had hitched it to a sort of V2 rocket.'

She was certainly not universally admired and many thought it shocking that someone like her should have the honour to be the first woman MP. Rebecca West wrote, 'It is difficult for many people to accept that when an electron is fired at a screen punched with two holes it passes through both, but not if they ever heard Lady Astor telling a story. She saw no reason why mutually exclusive statements should not both be true. Interesting as this turn of mind is, it may be doubted if most people would consider it desirable in a Member of Parliament.'

Winston Churchill was openly hostile to her and when Nancy asked why he replied, 'Because I find a woman's intrusion into the House of Commons as embarrassing as if she burst into my bathroom when I had nothing with which to defend myself, not even a sponge.' Nancy sweetly responded, 'Winston, you're not handsome enough to have worries of that kind.'

She had a love-hate relationship with Churchill all her life. Long before she became an MP she protested that 'in private conversation he tries on speeches like a man trying on bow ties in his bedroom to see how he would look in them'. On another, infuriated by something he said, she expostulated 'Winston, if you were my husband I should put poison in your coffee.' He shot back, 'Nancy, if you were my wife, I would drink it!'

In the 1930s Churchill had many critics, who called him rash, impetuous, tactless, contentious, inconsistent, forever out of step. One Tory MP told Nancy, 'I just don't know what to make of him.' She asked brightly, 'How about a nice rug?'

She had a headstrong and often chaotic approach to life which rubbed many of her colleagues up the wrong way. Sir Henry Channon fumed, 'How I loathe that interfering termagant.' Aneurin Bevan described her as 'America's revenge for George III.'

Field Marshal Montgomery once told her, 'I don't like women Members of Parliament' and she retorted tartly, 'Well, I don't like generals, with one exception. General Evangeline Booth (of the Salvation Army).' Monty was obliged to make a tactical retreat.

Nancy claimed she was terrified when she first entered the Chamber of the House of Commons and sat for five hours without moving. She had to clamber over the legs of male MPs to sit down – the bench system still perpetuates this ungainly experience for male and female alike – and the nearest lavatory to the Chamber which she could use was half a mile away. It is only now, in 1997, that the two Division lobbies have been equipped with ladies' lavatories.

She had a sharp sense of the ridiculous and could have made a fortune on the variety stage. Her mimicry was outstanding and her impersonations legendary. In 1963 she was interviewed on television and quite spontaneously made a brilliant caricature of Eleanor Roosevelt by placing the necklace of pearls she was wearing across her teeth and smiling wickedly. She was 84 at the time but behaved like a young girl.

Although she used her stage talents to good effect her speeches tended to be a 'jumble of *obiter dicta*'. A talent for witty interjection was indulged, sometimes to the amusement but more likely to the annoyance of speakers and audience alike. 'Nancy shut-up' was often heard but seldom heeded. Rebuked on one occasion, she protested she had been listening for hours before interrupting. 'Yes, we've HEARD you listening,' said one exasperated colleague, provoked beyond endurance.

She criticised members of her own party just as freely as those of others. Her views an all subjects were, more often than not, highly colourful.

'We have got to make the world safe for men. They have made it darn unsafe for us. The country has been in danger for 2,000 years – ever since men began to rule it alone . . . I haven't anything against men, but Eve showed which was the weaker.

'We have got to stop paying too much attention to the common man. It is the uncommon people who have achieved things. Although, as one of the common people myself, I like the common people, it is the uncommon people that I follow.'

She was an ardent feminist but also an intemperate advocate of temperance. Once, during a debate, she uttered the immortal words 'Gentlemen, I would rather commit adultery than let a drop of alcohol pass my lips.' To which came the fairly obvious retort, 'Who wouldn't?'

On one occasion, however, she did succumb to the demon drink. At the Midland Hotel in Manchester she swept everyone majestically in to lunch and invited the guests to choose their liquid refreshment. So as not to offend her sensibilities as a strict teetotaller, they all meekly plumped for lemonade. She, however, opted for cider apparently thinking it was merely fruit cordial and not alcoholic, and her guests gratefully followed suit. Her speech at an election meeting later that afternoon was even more spirited than usual.

She had a missionary streak which led to her moral, social and religious crusades. She fought the War Office because they had sanctioned the use of brothels by our troops in India. However, she was brilliantly out-manoeuvred every time by the Commander-in Chief, India. Whenever he received a cable about her Parliamentary Questions he immediately ordered the Military Police to close down all brothels at 10.00 p.m. that evening until 1.00 a.m. the following morning. That enabled him to cable the War Office in the following terms: 'A check on all brothels used by British troops in India at midnight has produced a nil return.'

Surprisingly she found herself more than once an object of moral suspicion. Seeing a young American looking at the outside of the House of Commons she said to him, 'Would you like to go in?' to which he answered, 'You are the sort of woman my mother told me to avoid.'

During the war Plymouth was the target of much German bombing and the civilian population laid much of the blame for this on the presence of the Navy in the city. In order to foster good relations between the two communities, Nancy persuaded the Commander-in-Chief of the Fleet to accompany her on a tour of the poor districts which had suffered worst. As a morale booster she suggested that the Commander wear his impressive full-dress uniform and she would dress as smartly as for the London Season. Together, in one of Plymouth's roughest districts, they approached a ramshackle house with boarded-up windows, evidently still occupied. After knocking several times a small boy answered. They asked if his mother and father were at home. He answered, 'Mother's out. It'll be all right if you go up but be sure to leave five shillings on the mantelpiece.' Clearly, the admiral was not the first sailor to call there with a pretty girl on his arm.

Nancy was fearless of all physical dangers, criticism and people. She once took on Mrs Pandit (Nehru's sister and India's High Commissioner in London), who was complaining about British colonisation in India, and told her bluntly, 'If it hadn't been for British rule in India you would have been burnt as a widow years ago.'

Michael Astor, writing about his mother with complete candour while she was still alive, described her 'disconcerting lack of scruple, which would show itself when her will was challenged . . . her occasional appearance of ruthlessness, which was elemental and unpremeditated.'

He also referred to her 'prodigious tactlessness which was the bane of her social life' and 'her overbearing desire to get her own way.' Her visits to him at Eton 'took the form of nerve-racking interludes which produced moments of acute embarrassment . . . In her eyes, all schoolboys were children and she was ready to appropriate any one of them; to seize a boy at random and ask if he had cleaned his teeth, said his prayers and written to his parents.' Apparently, his tutor 'lived in terror of meeting her' and was known, on hearing her voice wafting down the corridor, to crouch in a cupboard in his sitting room, being 'quietly asphyxiated by the fumes of his pipe until danger had passed'.

Capable of putting two fingers in her mouth and blowing a piercing whistle if she needed to attract attention, Lady Astor was, according to her lady's maid, a somewhat trying employer. She was capable of great generosity but also mean gestures like offering her maid chocolates she had already bitten and did not like, and ticking her off in front of strangers.

Kenneth Rose tells how Nancy determined, aged 70, to travel up to the north-west to support her godson, John Grigg, who stood as Conservative candidate for Oldham West in 1955. On hearing it was sometimes difficult to secure seats on railway trains, she dispatched several footmen in advance to occupy the corner seats until she and Kenneth Rose arrived.

Having skimmed through the papers and read a chapter or two from the Bible she turned, without a single pleasantry, to question the complete stranger in the adjacent seat about his religious beliefs, forcing him to retreat behind the protective barrier of the *Financial Times*.

The party then proceeded to Oldham West where Nancy gave 'as fierce a verbal battering as Socialism has ever received, including such references as: "Ramsay Macdonald once said to me he never knew what loyalty was – until he left the Labour party"' and (perhaps thinking of herself) 'The Tory Party always puts its problem members on the back benches. The Socialists put theirs on the Front Bench.' Despite her endeavours, Grigg lost by 4,000 votes.

Her skills as a hostess were legendary, both in London and at Cliveden where she entertained an eclectic mix of actors, politicians, diplomats, journalists, constituency workers etc. 'This house is like a huge liner and that woman is the rudder,' said her first child, Bobby Shaw. She was a vitalising genius at parties and gatherings, scattering wisecracks and personal remarks in all directions. 'It was her habit to greet guests, even those who had come to see her on serious matters, with a salvo of random rudeness accompanied by nods and becks and wreathèd smiles, a process which was made no more acceptable because she described it as "chaffin".'

She was no respecter of the Great and the Good. Sir Thomas Inskip, a Cabinet Minister of ample proportions, was staying at Cliveden and came down early for dinner. Nancy was reading her Bible by the fire and, unfortunately, Sir Thomas tripped over a light flex as he came into the room. 'Pick up your feet, you great hulk,' she said without looking up from her Bible.

Allegations of pro-Nazi sympathies at her weekend house parties at Cliveden in the 1930s were the unfounded inventions of the Communist journalist, Claud Cockburn. 'She was no Nazi sympathiser,' wrote her godson, John Grigg, 'she hated tyranny.' She often met Ribbentrop as German Ambassador socially in

London and bewildered him with her quick-fire irreverence towards Hitler. She made fun of the Führer's appearance and asked how anyone could be expected to take him seriously if he insisted on wearing a Charlie Chaplin moustache.

She treated Stalin with equal lack of deference. On a visit to the Soviet Union in 1931 she had frightened the wits out of the interpreters by asking him why he had slaughtered so many Russians. Stalin rose to the challenge and explained that some slaughter is inevitable when the constitution of a country is fundamentally disrupted, and that the violent death of a large number of people was necessary before the Communist State could be firmly established.

Her courage was admirable but her judgment often questionable. In 1936, when Hitler marched into the demilitarised Rhineland, she gave a dinner party at Cliveden where her distinguished guests were made to play musical chairs. The incident was recalled by Baroness Ravensdale, daughter of Lord Curzon, Foreign Secretary 1919-24: 'I could not believe my eyes when she made these illustrious statesmen play musical chairs after dinner. I thought the situation entirely mad. European politics were in front of me with Maisky the Russian Ambassador, Tituleseu the Romanian Ambassador, and Baron de Cartier de Marchienne the Belgian Ambassador, and many others fighting for chairs in a hideous nightmare of conflicting aims and certainly not for collective security. No one in the room wanted war; and yet what an ironical spectacle this was of M. Auriol, Secretary General to the League of Nations, Norman Davis the American delegate and the rest, all playing like spoilt children at a school treat, wrenching chairs away from each other. The German Ambassador must have thought the Führer could get away with anything after such an exhibition.'

She gave up her seat in 1945 at the request of her husband and described herself after retirement as an extinct volcano. But her aura remained at the Commons for some time after she had left. A succeeding lady MP remembers that when Nancy visited the Commons after her retirement, she never failed to visit the Lady Members' Room to leave a note to the effect that they were a useless bunch and didn't hit out hard enough.

She had done much, not least by her flamboyance and the exaggeration of her advocacy, to advance many changes for the better in the whole field of social welfare. If she attained no high office, or other conventional symbol of political success, it was because she was not credited with cool judgement, steadiness of course and discretion of tongue. But somehow she had a way of making those virtues seem second-class.

The variety of her excellence was impressive. Politician, hostess, mother of a large family, conversationalist, expert in mimicry and charade, formidable champion of assorted causes – anything you could do she could do better.

Alert and birdlike – always beautifully dressed, even in old age, she arrived at the salon of couturier Victor Stiebel when in her seventies. His collections were being shown to 30 or 40 silent women. 'I see,' she said loudly 'you're still making' hideous clothes for equally hideous women.' 'Yes,' said Stiebel, 'and it doesn't seem to me you are in any way out of place.' Nancy roared with laughter, not in the least offended by the put-down.

Providence could not have made a more exhilarating and provocative choice for the first woman to enter the House of Commons. It is a pity she did not achieve her ambition and be the first also to enter the Lords. Nancy was famous for her moral courage, social and athletic gifts and a warm and rumbustious personality.

She took regular exercise and a cold bath every morning. She kept her rooms a little colder than comfortable because 'I like to keep tough. I am an outdoor person.' Her physical fitness was useful during the war in providing inspiration to her shell-shocked constituents. On one occasion she went into an air-raid shelter where morale seemed rather low. She looked around and without saying a word did a tour, not walking but turning cartwheels and somersaults. She then cried to the astonished assembly 'Are we downhearted?' Amidst roars of approval she then walked back up the stairs to the street, where an air-raid was in progress.

'Beautiful, intelligent and witty, an uninhibited extrovert who insisted on being the centre of the stage, inexhaustible, pugnacious, she was of the right kind to be first to do anything.' On her last day in Westminster a fellow MP told her she would be missed. She said 'I'll miss the House. The House won't miss me. I've seen 'em all go – Lloyd George, Asquith, Baldwin, Snowden, Macdonald – and not one of 'em was missed. The House is like a sea. MPs are like little ships that sail across it and disappear over the horizon. Some of 'em carry a light. Others don't. That's the only difference.' Nancy's light still shines.

Cynthia Payne

'No sex please I'm the hostess.'
*****

It was a quintessentially English sex scandal. A brothel in a suburban semi, a retired squadron leader in a 'pinny', a Keystone Kops raid by policemen wearing wigs and other disguises . . . It was tailor-made for Sid James, Kenneth Williams and the entire *Carry On* cast.

Sex has never been taken entirely seriously in England. The eighteenth-century letter-writer, Lord Chesterfield, advised his son to avoid the temptations of prostitutes: 'The pleasure is transient, the expense exorbitant and the position ridiculous.' But he might have amended his advice, at least in part, if he had encountered Mrs Cynthia Payne.

The position was even more ridiculous than Lord Chesterfield could have envisaged. But Mrs Payne's pleasures were far from pricey – she even offered cheap rates for pensioners and the disabled. And the pleasure was permanent rather than transient. The entire nation has been chuckling for years over events which could happen only in England.

For a while, Cynthia Payne (changed from Paine for 'professional reasons') occupied a place in national affections only slightly below that of the Queen Mother.

'I do feel loved by the public. I haven't the love of a good man but I do have the love of the country. It has filled a void really and no one was more surprised than me.'

Nigel Dempster compared her with Margaret Thatcher. 'They are both domineering middle-aged women who are used to holding sway over a bunch of subservient and ostensibly respectable men. Mrs P calls them her slaves; to Mrs T they are known simply as The Cabinet.'

Cynthia had a hard childhood, shattered by the death of her mother when she was only eleven. She scarcely knew her father when he returned from the sea to look after his two young girls. She spent years unsuccessfully trying to win his approval. He was a pillar of Bognor Regis society, a Freemason, and impossible to please. 'He was always running me down. He thought I'd turn out no good. His death (nearly 20 years ago now) released me mentally. I likened it to a gay finally coming out of the closet. That's what I did.'

Her early life was chequered by a variety of inadequate men, times of desperate poverty and a series of back-street abortions. She gave up being a prostitute 'I was never any good in bed – I talked too much.'

She did a stretch of six months in prison (reduced from a sentence of 18) under a statute of 1750 for keeping a disorderly house and controlling prostitutes. She could probably have avoided prison by pleading 'not guilty' but she was not prepared to do so because details of her 'guests' would have come into the public domain and many of them were notables – she claims MPs and judges amongst their number.

In 1976 she rented premises in the West End, operating a brothel five afternoons a week. But the police spoilt that one day by breaking the door down and bursting in uninvited. They knew it was a knocking shop but didn't have the elementary good manners to knock before entering.

This distasteful experience prompted a move to the more genteel ambience of 32 Ambleside Avenue, Streatham – superficially, at any rate, an unlikely venue for 'The House of a Thousand and One Delights'. However, the 'delights' were later described as being akin to a vicarage tea party with sex thrown in at the end. As Mrs Payne helpfully confides: 'The secret of a good party lies in the combination of people and, if sex is on the menu, you've got a party.' With an eye to the proprieties, she was always determined that the parties should be more than the sum of the private parts. One can almost hear her say, like Professor Higgins' Eliza: 'I'm a respectable girl, I am.'

Accustomed to human nature in all its infinite variety, only two customers (she prefers to call them guests) raised her eyebrows by their requests. One was a gentleman of 55 who wanted to be dressed as a baby – nappies, pins and all – and tucked up in bed with a bottle of warm milk, which he thoughtfully provided for himself. Madame Cyn drew the curtains and returned in half an hour. Harmless pleasure.

Then there was the bank manager from the Midlands (as opposed to the Midland) who wanted to be plastered with mud. That stumped Madame Cyn at first. Where do you find mud in the suburbs, with all that tarmac around? Then she had a brainwave! Of course. The Hoover! In a trice the man was transmogrified into a glistening bank manager. Cyn first coated him with baby oil and then emptied the contents of the Hoover all over his body. That apparently did the trick and off he went, as ecstatic as a Flanders and Swann hippopotamus.

Cynthia saw herself as an arm (or other anatomical part) of the Welfare State – filling gaps in the Social Services network. She catered almost exclusively for older men and helped a large number of disabled men. She rightly felt they needed her talents more than the younger, able-bodied ones.

Her suburban sin factory was never a vulgar exercise in money-grubbing. In fact she never sought to make money from her parties. In any case, by the time she had paid for the girls and the refreshments (not to mention the Hoover bags and baby oil) there was nothing left for her. She did it for the pleasure it gave to others, which gave pleasure to her.

Her most arresting (literally) innovation was the Luncheon Voucher Scheme. Men paid from £8 to £25 for a counterfeit-proof 20 year old Luncheon Voucher which then entitled them to food (usually sandwiches made by Cynthia), drink, a striptease and a trip to bed with a willing woman.

In 1980 she had an End of Film Party to celebrate completion of the film based on her life called *Personal Services*. It was so successful that the London Borough of Merton felt obliged to change the name of its Personal Services Unit to the Housing & Social Services Department to avoid confusion.

She was furious when the police (many flourishing cameras), in an incident reminiscent of the Keystone Kops, raided the party which led to her trial. 'How dare they come in, knock doors down and ruin a nice party? There were men in wheelchairs there.'

In fact all human life was there as well:

The Director of the film, Mr Terry Jones, (formerly a member of the Monty Python team), was present, 'getting the vibes' according to Madam Cyn. Also a young man called Keith, dressed as a French Maid. And a man called Sid, no doubt getting his share.

There were also one or two unwelcome guests – policemen from the vice squad who had tricked their way in by deceiving Madam Cyn. One disguised himself by dyeing his beard white and carrying a walking stick; the other tried to make himself look inconspicuous with effeminate clothing, eye make-up and a monocle! The former greeted Cynthia with a bunch of roses, a box of hand-made chocolates and a kiss on the hand – *Et tu Brute!*

The trial itself was high farce. When asked in Court about some garden canes which had been seized she candidly admitted that some were, yes, for tomatoes, but the others were for the slaves.

Some men, apparently, get their kicks by serving a very difficult mistress. Cynthia satisfied this urge in her slaves by wearing very high heels ('They were usually killing me') while they Hoovered around and generally tidied up her house. As a special treat she also gave them a 'little bit of caning, insulting and mild humiliation.' She had difficulty, however, in keeping slaves for any length of time: 'I'm not really strict enough. I get too friendly with them.'

Lifting the veil further, she revealed to the Court: 'No. Slaves are not interested in sexual intercourse. It would be like growing spuds in a Ming vase.'

A slave is always male. She had one slave who came round every Monday for 20 years. 'Just to excite him I would put my high heeled shoes in the entrance hall and leave a cane leaning beside them. All slaves like high-heeled shoes, the higher the better.' But it became a bit of a fag to wear high heels every Monday morning so she stopped. The Monday masochist moped around mournfully for a few weeks and, when he pointed out it wasn't much to ask in exchange for all the cleaning she thought to herself 'twirl out those high heels again – it's better than doing your own housework.'

Naturally, slaves were not invited to the parties themselves. Anything so pleasurable would have made them very miserable. But they were permitted to come round afterwards because 'they were very good at clearing up'.

Some of her guests were game enough to show up at her trial in her support. One 85 year old said he went to the parties for social rather than sexual pleasure. 'In my old age life is rather dull and these parties were very jolly. They made me feel younger and that was rather nice.'

Even at the peak of her partying career, Madam Cyn says she only gave three or four parties a year. They took so much planning she could not cope with any more. Cynthia neither smokes nor drinks heavily. She keeps cats and shops at Safeway. Her home was no brothel, she said, but a place for private gatherings of friends.

Apparently, she never had time for sex at her own parties because she was 'too busy making the sandwiches, seeing they don't drink too much and making sure they don't put cigarette burns on the carpet'.

She makes the kinky and bizarre sound as everyday as beans on toast. 'I tell you dearie, its a lot of hard mental work doing all that bondage. I've found it particularly boring.

'All that caning is ridiculous. I blame the public schools. Never send your kids to a single sex school.' She claims she would have been bored stiff doing the caning all on her own. She invited friends round to help out. 'Come on dear, pop upstairs and give him six whacks of the cane. Then we'll all have some poached eggs on toast and a cup of tea.'

Mrs Payne deliberately makes no critical judgments and talks about her parties as if she were peddling Tupperware. She affects a charming innocence about the whole scene, but is aware of her own celebrity.

She recalls that one day, while struggling with her shopping in Knightsbridge, her acute senses picked up the gaze ('I'm sure I know that face from somewhere') of a well-dressed gentleman. He was in a car stopped by the traffic lights and turned out to be Prince Charles, whose intense stare turned to a scarlet flush of embarrassment when he realised just who he was staring at – much to the delight of Madame Cyn and HRH's bodyguards.

Eventually, bored with sex, and looking for a career move, Cynthia turned to politics under the slogan 'Vote for me or I'll give you ten of the best.'

She stood, as Leader of the Payne and Pleasure Party, in the 1988 Kensington by-election on a platform of legalised and wholesome prostitution. 'The people of England need to know about our archaic sex laws. Only the people of England can change them.' Kensington seemed like a good place to start.

'When I was imprisoned in 1980, the British public was in uproar. People don't know our sex laws; most of them were made by men for men in the eighteenth century. It isn't illegal for a man to go to a brothel, but they can put the girl or madam into prison. It isn't very fair or logical is it?'

She was confident of winning and bet £70 on herself at odds of 5,000 to one against. Also, just in case, she bet £50 at 20 to 1 on that she would get at least 1,000 votes. If all her bets had come home she would have made a tidy profit of around £350,000. She thought every man in the world should vote for her on her ticket to legalise brothels but, leaving nothing to chance, she kept herself busy kissing everyone in sight in exchange for votes.

Sadly, the Conservative Party candidate spoilt her dream by winning. But she outpolled Screaming Lord Sutch by a margin of three to one. Her defeat was Westminster's loss – she would have been a hugely entertaining figure at the Gothic Palace of Varieties. She would, of course, have been a fabulously strict Madam Speaker and could have taught the Whips' Offices a thing or two about discipline. She would have provided much merriment and diversion for those endless summer all-night sittings, finding plenty of 'guests' for her parties, which would have whiled away the hours between votes.

I am not sure that Cynthia is actually a Battleaxe at all. Like many in her profession, she has a heart of gold burnished by daily contact with human nature in the raw.

Meeting her recently at a party she handed me her visiting card on which she had naughtily scribbled 'To Christine, I am so sorry to lose one of my best girls.' I was fractionally concerned to discover she had also given one to my husband which said 'To Neil, I am so sorry to lose one of my best customers.'

Fanny Cradock

(b.1909 – d.1994)

'I have always been extremely rude and I have always got exactly what I wanted.'

*****

Fanny Cradock was not the first TV cook, but she was the undisputed doyenne of the genre in the Fifties and Sixties. She was a Battleaxe beyond compare – the acme of imperious irascibility. Elizabeth David taught *haute cuisine* to the middle classes but Fanny Cradock brought 'haughty cuisine' to the masses.

Doubt never entered her kitchen. 'I have always been extremely rude and I have always got exactly what I wanted.'

Fanny was invariably accompanied, as a side-dish, by her husband Johnnie – monocled, moustached and monosyllabic. Together they brought 'a dash of pre-war upper-class raffishness to the simple business of cooking an omelette'. They bore a striking resemblance to the Osbert Lancaster caricatures, Lord and Lady Littlehampton, and might well have escaped from one of his Pocket Cartoons. Their first live cookery programme, called *Kitchen Magic*, went out in 1955.

Dressed with preposterous incongruity in evening gown and dinner jacket for the manufacture of even the messiest meals, they consciously combined *haute couture* and *haute cuisine*. Aprons were definitely for housemaids. The overall effect was a kind of cross between Dame Barbara Cartland and Danny La Rue.

Her authoritative manner convinced the viewer unconsciously that cooking in full Hartnell gown and diamonds, make-up applied with a trowel, and looking for all the world as though departing for a Covent Garden gala performance, was natural, practical, even desirable. Had it not been too absurd even for her, Fanny would clearly have worn three-quarter length white kid gloves.

She claimed her mode of dress derived from going to live with her grandmother at the age of 15, after being expelled from school for encouraging other girls to contact the spirit world ('I was on intimate terms with the court of Louis XIV').

As part of the bargain it was her duty to cook dinner. But grandmama stipulated that she had to be in evening dress in her place at the table by the time the dish was served. 'To save time I wore my Schiaparelli beaded frock and slave bangles in the kitchen – that's how I learnt to cook in ballgowns.'

On television Fanny engulfed the viewer in a flood-tide of chatter, delivered in a gravel-throated voice, once described as sounding like 'a circular saw going through a sheet of gin-soaked cardboard'.

Johnnie, a decent, kindly but rather hopeless old cove stood deferentially and discreetly one pace behind her and she rewarded his dog-like devotion by huskily roaring commands at him: 'Johnnie, frying pan . . . Johnnie, more wine . . . Johnnie, more butter . . . don't stint.' He had a great gift for silence but did once utter a memorable valediction to the viewers: 'May all your doughnuts look like Fanny's.' It was a more innocent age.

Forties food in Britain was frightful – fuel rather than frills. A rationed diet of dried egg, whale meat and Spam did not make for an encouraging start. In the upper echelons of Society one did one's best with limited materials. For instance, the menu at the Strand Palace Hotel during the war included: (a) 'Ballotine de Jambon Valentoise' and (b) 'Assiette froide et salade'. The authorised translation by the management was (a) Hot Spam and (b) Cold Spam.

But, even if fine ingredients were available, contemporary culinary practice usually wrecked them. Today we roast lamb at 15 minutes per pound and serve it a succulent pink. In 1945 it was roasted at 35 minutes per pound to a texture of dry, grey cardboard.

Fanny recalled how, during the war, 'our cooking used to amaze our friends. They thought we had black market supplies from Fortnum's.' She was a master of disguises. 'Bracken shoots were asparagus and I used liquid paraffin for my pastry. We caught and cooked sparrows from the garden and often ate baked hedgehogs (rather like frog's legs).'

She was self-taught and claimed to have learnt much from her grandmother. She also picked up a great deal as a child by going into hotel kitchens, where she was perched up on a shelf, legs dangling, to watch the chefs in the south of France where the family wintered. While her father gambled the family into penury in the casino, her mother dallied with admirers, who paid the young Fanny to leave them alone.

She was born Phyllis Pechey in the Channel Islands in 1909. Her mother was a singer and actress; her father, a lepidopterist who wrote novels, plays and pantomimes. He did not radiate warmth to his young offspring. Fanny recalled: 'Father used to say to Mother "Why not send those two children of yours out to play on the railway!"'

She claimed that, by the time she was 14, she was engaged to three young men. At 16 she eloped and married one of them. At 17 she was a pregnant widow. Her first husband joined the RAF and was killed four months later in an accident. When she was 19 her father was adjudged bankrupt and Fanny was reduced to scratching a living by washing up in a Roman Catholic canteen. To make ends meet she also sold vacuum cleaners door-to-door and demonstrated Swiss roll mix. This latter experience was to prove its worth in her first television programme, when she demonstrated how to produce Swiss roll, eclairs and souffle-en-surprise for eight people for 6 shillings and two pence farthing.

Her second husband was cast into outer darkness and never mentioned. Her third husband, Old Harrovian Johnnie, she met in 1939 during a blackout on Hackney Marshes. Johnnie lifted Fanny out of actual and into relative poverty, as his definition of hardship was having to do without cigars. Although she took his name and they remained inseparable until his death in 1987, they lived in sin until 1977.

By this stage eccentricity had graduated to confusion of memory. She told the Registrar that her maiden name was de Peche, rather than Pechey, and that she was only 55, a somewhat improbable calculation as her elder son was then 50.

In claimed infallibility, Fanny's *ex-culina* advice rivalled the *ex-cathedra* pronouncements of the Pope. The detail was often highly eccentric. She enjoined the viewer to use 'mushroom seeds' (overlooking that mushrooms don't seed). She advised that soy sauce came from India, that 'haggis' derived from the Abruzzi (a region of central Italy) and that gazpacho was a non-alcoholic beverage suitable for drinking with hors d'oeuvres!

Most memorable of all, she created a patterned jelly dish and promoted it with gusto as 'Jelly à la Zizi,' under the innocent misapprehension that 'zizi' was the French word for 'diagonal stripes'. In fact, it is French slang for the male member – the 'willy' not the MP!

Fanny and Johnnie's double-act enthralled and delighted television audiences from the Fifties onwards. Fanny's forceful and colourful personality offered a welcome antidote to the drabness and austerity of post-war Britain. She enjoined the British housewife to divest herself of her culinary prejudices and overcome her 'greatest handicap, the British husband – who just wants what Mum used to make'.

Ever full of good tips, she advised viewers to adopt 'the third ballet position' to avoid spilling soup. She incurred the wrath of the Scottish fishing industry in 1974 when she demonstrated how to make fake scampi with cheap monkfish and caused a collapse in the demand for the real thing.

Fanny went to almost any lengths in search of greater professionalism. She even had plastic surgery on her Roman nose when her producer hinted it was too big and was 'casting shadows on the food'.

In 1956 the French chef, Raymond Oliver, threw down the gauntlet, declaring that women were inferior to men in the kitchen. Fanny picked up the glove without hesitation and challenged him to a televised culinary duel at the Café Royal. Unfairly for her, but typically French and chauvinist, Oliver had made it clear to the organisers in advance that she was not to be permitted to win (which she clearly did on points) and it was declared a diplomatic draw.

Fanny's fearsome delivery might have put a Gorgon to flight. But she suffered un-Battleaxy nerves before facing the cameras for the initial programme. She had to retreat to a local church to pray for 20 minutes before going on. Johnnie, also terrified, simply froze and had to be physically pushed by a technician onto the set, accompanied by the stage whisper: 'Get a move on, you silly sod, you're on.'

The producer of the show said she was often so petrified before a performance that her eyes would bulge and she would fix her guests with a terrifying stare, frightening them half to death. Sir Gerald Kelly, President of the Royal Academy, was so unnerved by her presence he could not utter a single word. Exasperated, she commanded him, 'For God's sake say something, even if it's only goodbye.' He promptly obeyed, thankful to escape his ordeal!

Off-camera the irascible grand dame of the British kitchen was a crashing snob and an Olympic gold medallist at tantrum-throwing. Her literary agent, Rosemary Bromley, said, 'She behaved appallingly but she was unique'. A fellow food writer said 'Let's be honest. I couldn't stand the woman. She was always so rude to Johnnie. The local shops used to hate it when she came in.' Neighbours complained of her as a terrible woman with a tendency to lash out at all and sundry with her walking stick if they got in her way. Said one, 'She took a swipe at my legs yesterday when I tried to speak to her as she was walking her dog Mia, a tiny white Chinese Shi-Tzu. She glared then growled at me to shut up and go away.'

Fanny boasted of her public altercations, many of which involved cars. On one occasion some youths refused to move their car which was in her way. 'I went in kicking low. I can still remember how exhilarating was the slosh of handbag on fleshy nose.' They moved the car.

Arrested in 1964 for careless driving, the officer described her as 'abusive and excited'. Asking her to move her Rolls-Royce, which was parked across a stream of traffic, she abused him as a 'uniformed delinquent', telling him to wait while she finished her conversation. When she did finally move her car she reversed into the car behind, roundly blaming the officer. 'I was just doing as I was told – you told me to back up.'

In 1983, after following her grandmother's advice to chauffeurs to 'stick to the middle of the road', she swerved into another car. Yelling at the innocent driver 'How dare you hit my car!' she drove off. Honking and flashing his lights, he gave chase for 15 miles, eventually overtook her and attempted to flag her down by standing in front of her car, waving his arms like a windmill. This was a painful misjudgment on his part. She ran him over, claiming in court that the other driver's threatening behaviour had made her afraid to stop.

In addition to the police and law enforcers, she also had spectacular rows with the Inland Revenue and with ordinary members of the general public who had committed high crimes and misdemeanours such as daring to call her Fanny instead of Mrs Cradock.

She was finally taken off the menu by the BBC in 1987 for exploding in front of a studio audience at an inoffensive presenter, Pamela Armstrong. The poor girl had merely wandered over to see what was cooking but Fanny screamed at her 'Nobody, but nobody goes onto my set. I have never seen such a bloody shambles in all my life' – adding more volcanic expletives as she gathered momentum. Explaining her absence as illness, she was retired on the spot.

Fanny was a prolific journalist and her Bon Viveur column in the *Daily Telegraph* lasted for many years. The *Telegraph*, sticklers for exactitude, wanted it to be called 'Bon Vivant' but she overruled them, demonstrating a sure but surprising common touch. She also wrote a pseudonymous column for the *Daily Mail* as Francis Dale, and a 'Hair and Beauty' column for the *Telegraph* as Elsa Frances.

She heaped abuse on everyone from fellow television presenters and journalists to Margaret Thatcher whom she described as 'wearing cheap shoes and clothes'.

Other cookery writers were the subject of particularly vitriolic attention. The cookery books she owned and used were covered with waspish pencil comments. She scrawled all over *The Cooking of Provincial France* by MFK Fisher with her vituperative pencil, displaying not just her culinary prejudices in the margins. To the hapless American author she thundered, 'You are supposed to be writing about France, the centre of the fashionable world, not America, the master ruiners of food.' Prompted by a suggestion that virgin olive oil should be used in a recipe: 'The only virgins in France are little girls and most are very little indeed.'

She died in 1994 in a Sussex nursing home. Defying pneumonia, the last dish she ever cooked was caramelised onion tart. An obituarist wrote that 'The Cradocks' secret was the snobbery and pretension of the times. In the post-war era they made their hungry, servantless readers and viewers feel they still belonged to an elite.' Another described her as 'A preposterous character, the foodie you loved to loathe.'

She was stylish to the last. A short time before she died a friend took her out of the nursing home for lunch. As he shook her by her gloved hand she winced with pain. He said, 'I'm terribly sorry. Is it arthritis?' She was most indignant. 'Certainly not. It's the diamonds, my darling. Just the diamonds.'

Bubbles Rothermere

Viscountess 'Bubbles' Rothermere

(b.1929 – d.1992)

'So great was her love of parties that she would attend the opening of an envelope.'

*****

Marx may not immediately spring to mind when conjuring up a vision of 'Bubbles' Rothermere. But Marx described her to a 'T': 'Effervescent? Did you know me ven I effer vosn't?' (The joke was Groucho's, naturally. Karl's punch lines tended to be less pithy – it took 75 years for the penny to drop in Soviet Russia).

Bubbles had a surprising amount in common with Lenin and Stalin too. Like them she was a great party leader. But her parties were more amusing – and the death toll was much lower. Britain's 'New Labour' Party has learned a lot from her also – in particular that champagne is more fun than dialectical materialism.

Lord Rothermere announced his support for Tony Blair in the 1997 General Election, recently having converted to champagne socialism. This news was received with mixed feelings in New Labour's Walworth Road HQ on two counts. First, as a peer, his Lordship didn't have a vote. Second, and more seriously, anyone still talking in obsolete terms of 'socialism' in any form excited the deepest suspicion. It is probably just as well that Bubbles did not live to see Blairite Britain, as polenta and fizzy water were never exactly her preferred pabulum.

She was not a Battleaxe in the conventional sense – but she was unconventional in many senses, battling her way from birth as plain Patricia Evelyn Beverley Matthews to become the vivacious Viscountess, whose lifelong social stamina sustained her through an Olympic relay-race of parties, small talk, cocktails and canapés.

Born in 1929 she was early considered a beauty. Under the stage name of Beverley Brooks she took up acting. 'All the World's a Stage,' thought Bubbles, 'and I want to be a star.' Her only role of note was Sally, girlfriend of Kenneth More playing the part of legendary legless air-ace Douglas Bader in the 1956 film *Reach for the Sky*.

Voted one of the 10 most beautiful women in London in 1955, she quickly divorced her first husband and announced that, next time, she wanted someone rich. She heard that Vere Harmsworth was on the loose. Patricia, with total self-conviction, believed she could make something happen if she willed it enough. She set her cap at Vere, hooked him and announced contentedly, 'I married an empire.'

She was a true British eccentric – her ample form was festooned in a multitude of expensive fabrics, bedecked in a shock of colours clashing like cymbals. She became as essential an ingredient of the London social scene as sugar in a champagne cocktail. Her irrepressible, outrageous presence enlivened all gatherings. Nicknamed 'Bubbles' on account of her love of champagne, she was a connoisseur of impeccable taste: often spotted with a glass of pink Dom Perignon in one hand and plain Louis Roederer in the other. She always wielded a swizzle stick as a prophylactic against the perennial peril – wind caused by imbibing an excess of champagne bubbles.

Her total disregard for the first half of the old adage 'You can never be too thin or too rich' was an inspiration to all believers in feminine curves. She refused to be tyrannised by the dogma of dieting and the vogue for cocktail-stick insects as models for clothes. She was a cheerleader for those who wanted FUN without worrying about pounds and ounces – or pounds and pence.

In this last respect she reminds me of the late, great multi-millionaire, Nubar Gulbenkian, who also believed wealth was to be enjoyed. Fed up with London traffic congestion, he bought a black taxicab and had it customised by a leading firm of Rolls-Royce coach-builders, observing proudly, 'They tell me it will turn on a sixpence – whatever that may be!'

Bubbles was the butt of ridicule from some women who felt less secure in themselves, their figures and their position in society. She was happy with all three and wanted everyone to know it.

Sartorially most startling, her typical Battledress extruded layers of frills and flounces – more reminiscent of Violet Elizabeth Bott (*Just William*'s girlfriend) than a Society hostess of a certain age. Adorned in taffeta and velvet, bows and layers, she burst forth like a bunch of blowzy dahlias. One commentator unkindly said she sometimes appeared to be wearing the entire Zandra Rhodes frock collection one on top of another, sometimes with plimsolls underneath and her leg in plaster for no apparent reason.

It was said that 'so great was her love of parties that she would attend the opening of an envelope'. She acted as a Pied Piper, calling her friends to bashes and thrashes. A 'brilliantly dotty, shimmeringly exotic night figure,' her presence could not be ignored at any party. She demanded to be, and usually was, the centre of attraction. Like an earthquake, her arrival in a room was preceded by tremors of growing intensity.

She aimed to turn life into a perpetual party, unencumbered by philosophical pretensions. Grand, witty and vivacious, she was a colourful, garish and charismatic figure. She attracted an eclectic gallimaufry of guests – actors, models, writers, peers, royalty, musicians, politicians, cockney car dealers and Hollywood stars. She had a marvellous sense of mischief and, if a diversion were needed, she would provide a *Girls' Own* schoolgirl jape – like expeditions in a fleet of Bentleys to an East End fish and chip shop to enjoy a midnight feast in the back of the car.

There came a time when Bubbles had still not appeared in *Hello!* magazine but many of her friends had. Feeling, as one would, something of a social outcast because of this, she contacted the magazine and asked if they would be interested in doing a piece about her. 'Of course' was the instant response 'What angle could we follow – do you have any animals?' 'No' said Bubbles 'but I will get some immediately.' Her secretary was instantly dispatched to purchase suitable canine accoutrements and Bubbles happily posed with them as lifelong friends.

Her married life did not follow the text-book. Friends said Vere could not live with her because she was too selfish and self-centred. When he inherited in 1978 he became a tax exile and lived in Paris, with a Korean inamorata, Maiko Lee. This was a cause of sadness to Bubbles but colonial life, even if only in France, did not appeal to her and she opted to stay in London, thus creating a somewhat unconventional marriage.

She could be self-indulgent, acerbic and antagonistic if provoked. She once saw her husband holding the hand of an attractive young female executive at the *Mail*'s annual staff party at Claridge's. The victim recalled that Vere 'had simply absent-mindedly forgotten to let go' after shaking her hand but Bubbles thought otherwise and hurled herself across the room 'like a black taffeta cannonball', hitting the young girl for six.

She was a determined worker for charity and many of her parties were not purely hedonistic, but raised money for a worthy cause. She exploited to the full the maxim that there is no such thing as a free lunch, and her guests frequently paid heavily to charity for her lavish hospitality.

Despite the fact that her villa where she died at Cap d'Ail once belonged to Greta Garbo, she hated being alone. She was almost always surrounded by a *galère* of attractive young men who would follow her like seagulls in the wake of a liner. One of them had the vital responsibility of carrying the plastic bag which contained her own personal supply of champagne.

No one was a more expert judge of the metropolitan social scene. At its glittering first-night she predicted the failure of Regine's, a nightclub in the roof garden of Derry & Toms, in Kensington. 'This place will never last,' she said. 'It's too far out of London.' It was almost a mile from Hyde Park Corner.

She gave herself selflessly to produce an heir for her husband. She had one daughter by her first marriage. Difficult pregnancies produced two more daughters by Vere. After the birth of her second daughter, both received absolution on the operating table, as neither was expected to survive. After the third daughter was born she was warned by the medics that it was too dangerous to try again for the coveted heir to the viscountcy. Despite that, she was determined to succeed, even at the risk of her own life. Jonathan finally arrived three years later, surviving only by a miracle.

Alas, poor Bubbles would not live to see the Millennium. She had oft expressed the view that she would like to see it in by holding 'a fantastic party on the rooftops with an amazing band. It would be fabulous and gay, with dancing on the top of skyscrapers.' One imagines her as Mary Poppins with guests following her, dancing from scraper to scraper on a cloud of champagne bubbles.

She died aged 63 from heart disease, exacerbated by an accidental drug overdose, in the South of France on 12 August 1992. True to form, only hours before her death she had frantically been telephoning to arrange More Parties, More Parties.

She was a free and generous soul. At her Memorial Service, the Rector of St Bride's, Fleet Street, paid a tribute to 'her love and natural kindness . . . her vivacity, sense of fun and quality of life enhancement.' Her husband observed she 'lived her life somewhat like a fighter pilot, throwing herself into situations that would daunt most of us.' Her epitaph? *Reach for the Sky*; the theme tune of which was played at her memorial service which was filled with the laughter, humour and the sense of fun which dominated her life.

Queen Victoria
(b.1819 – d.1901)

'Please understand that there is no one depressed in this house; we
are not interested in the possibilities of defeat; they do not exist.'
*****

In 1817 Queen Victoria's father, Edward Augustus, HRH the Duke
of Kent, became a prince of wails: 'God only knows the sacrifice it
will be . . . to become a married man. It is now seven and twenty
years that Mme. St Laurent and I have lived together: we are the
same age, and have been in all climates and difficulties together,
and you may imagine the pang it will occasion me to part with her
. . . She is of very good family and has never been an actress.'

What occasioned this outburst? The Prince Regent's only
daughter, Princess Charlotte, had just died unexpectedly aged
twenty-one. Charlotte's death meant there was not a single
legitimate heir among any of seventy-nine year old George III's
twelve children.

The Royal Family was ideal tabloid material. 'The King was
mad, the Princess of Wales was bad, the six Princes were wild and
the five Princesses were, in all but habit, nuns.' The succession
to the throne was in doubt and it was essential that George III's
sons should regularise their private lives and produce legitimate
heirs. Assorted mistresses and illegitimate children simply would
not do.

George III's twelve children had signally failed, as late as 1817, to secure the royal line, so the Duke of Kent was persuaded to do his duty. Mme. de St Laurent was regretfully discarded and entered a convent, and in May 1818 he married Princess Victoria of Saxe-Coburg, a thirty-two-year old widow with two children. Twelve months later she gave birth to the princess who was destined to become Queen Victoria. Then, as though exhausted by his exertions, within seven months the Duke of Kent was dead.

Princess Victoria was a strong personality from the start. Her father said, 'The little one is a pocket Hercules rather than a pocket Venus.' From infancy she showed signs of imperiousness arising from her rank. An exasperated music master told her, 'There is no royal road to music, Princess. You must practise like everybody else.' Victoria slammed the piano-lid with a bang and said 'There! you see there is no MUST about it.'

Even whilst a toddler she understood the gulf between royalty and a commoner: a playmate, Lady Jane Elliot, tried to play with some of Victoria's toys, evoking a response from the six-year-old princess worthy of Queen Elizabeth I in her prime: 'You must not touch those, they are mine; and I may call you Jane but you must not call me Victoria.'

Her ultra-possessive mother schemed to become the power behind the throne and subjected Victoria to suffocatingly close control. Only five days before her eighteenth birthday the King offered her a private income of £10,000 a year and full independence from her mother. She coerced Victoria into signing a letter accepting the money but refusing the independence, saying she wanted to remain with her 'dear mother'.

But upon her Accession in 1837, Victoria instantly showed that she intended to rule, even though she was only just eighteen. Her mother had hitherto scarcely allowed the Princess an hour of solitude in her rigidly controlled life. As Queen, however, Victoria commanded that her bed be removed immediately to another part of the palace, well away from her mother's bedroom, which she had previously been forced to share.

Throughout her long reign she subordinated the convenience of others to her own and, on the few occasions when thwarted, she flew into uncontrollable rages. An Indian servant, Abdul Karim, became her constant companion after 1887 and even taught her to speak Hindustani. The Ladies and Gentlemen of the Household, however, refused to associate with him because he was low-caste, objectionable and said to have contracted VD. But the Queen would have none of this.

When she decided that Abdul should accompany her on holiday in the South of France it was the last straw for the Household – because he would have to travel and eat with them. Lady Harriet Phipps had the unenviable task of presenting the Queen with an ultimatum – choose either Abdul or the Household. The Queen stormed around in a rage and swept her arm across her writing desk, sending the crowded paraphernalia – papers, pens, inkwell, Disraeli's jewelled dagger and all – crashing to the floor. The Prime Minister, Lord Salisbury, had to be summoned to persuade her that the French might think Abdul's position 'odd' and make 'rude remarks' about her. Abdul did not join the royal caravanserai but, to the despair of the Household, she ensured that he turned up later by ordinary train, and the rows continued all year.

Right from the start she was just as determined to show the politicians who was boss. Her first Prime Minister, Lord Melbourne, was a nineteenth-century lookalike of a New Labour leader – 'head of a weak Whig government, whilst holding Tory views himself he felt no sympathy for the Radicals amongst his followers.' He romanced the Queen and she was distraught when his government fell, following a defeat in Parliament in 1839.

Melbourne's successor, Sir Robert Peel, was a Tory and proposed to change some of the Whig ladies of the Queen's Household to demonstrate her confidence in the government. Victoria flexed her muscles and absolutely refused to change any. She wrote to Melbourne: 'The Queen of England will not submit to such trickery' and '. . . they wish to treat me like a girl but I will show them I am Queen of England.' As a result Peel refused to form a government and Melbourne was recalled.

In affairs of state she was firm, but in affairs of the heart she still fluttered as much as any young girl of twenty. She had to make a formal Declaration of Marriage to the assembled Privy Council. The

Duchess of Gloucester asked if she was nervous at the prospect. Victoria said 'Yes, but I did a much more nervous thing a little while ago. I proposed to Prince Albert.' (It had been impossible for Albert to take the initiative on account of his lower rank).

Albert had also been nervous about the engagement at first, writing that 'Victoria is said to be incredibly stubborn and her obstinacy constantly at war with her good nature . . . These are gloomy prospects.' Victoria, for her part, worried that she would not wear the trousers. 'I have always had my own way . . . Suppose he should endeavour to thwart me and oppose me in what I like, what a dreadful thing it would be.'

The Archbishop of Canterbury asked Victoria whether she wanted to alter the part of the marriage ceremony containing the promise to obey. She replied 'though not as Queen, as a woman she was ready to promise all things contained in this portion of the Liturgy.' Despite this, shortly after their marriage Albert was lamenting 'I am only the husband and not the master in the house.'

Victoria was proud of her exalted station and would not tolerate interference in her power of decision. On the other hand Albert refused to take orders from her. She had promised to obey him, yet she stubbornly insisted that he should obey her as Queen. There was an impasse at first but, until his death in 1861, they did develop a *modus vivendi* as Victoria became more and more dependent on the husband she adored.

She expressed her belief in his absolute perfection in the most cloying terms: 'I am grateful for possessing (really without vanity or flattery or blindness) the most perfect being as a husband in existence or who ever did exist; and I doubt whether anybody ever did love or respect another as I do my dear Angel.' Albert was more matter-of-fact: 'Victoria has greatly improved and has become very reasonable and good-natured.'

After 1861 her love blossomed into idolatry as she worshipped his memory. Someone suggested to Disraeli on his deathbed in 1881 that he might like to be visited by the Queen. But he replied, 'No it is better not. She would only ask me to take a message to Albert!' On another occasion, when Lady Beaconsfield suggested that 'The Prince of Wales must be a great comfort', Victoria merely snorted,

'Comfort! Why I caught him smoking a fortnight after his dear father died.'

For years after Albert's death she retired into seclusion as the Widow of Windsor, even refusing to open Parliament. In 1866, at last prevailed upon to do so once again, she described it as 'a dreadful ordeal which I can only compare to an execution'. She refused to drive in the State coach or wear the Robes of State, which were merely draped over the throne. Nor would she consent to read the Queen's Speech itself. She simply sat rigidly, staring in front of her whilst the Lord Chancellor performed the task. Next day she was 'terribly shaken, exhausted and unwell from the violent nervous shock' the effort had cost her. Even after a quarter of a century, at the Golden Jubilee in 1887, she refused to ride in the state coach wearing the Robes of State and crown. She insisted on riding in an open landau wearing a black silk dress and ordinary bonnet trimmed with white lace.

Despite her morbid Albertine neuroses she never abandoned her autocratic tendencies – she merely bent them to preserving Albert's memory, taking decisions according to his supposed wishes. In the complicated Schleswig-Holstein dispute in 1863 (basically between Denmark and Prussia) Victoria knew Albert would wish to preserve British neutrality. The Prime Minister, Lord Palmerston, believed in gunboat diplomacy and wanted to help gallant little Denmark against bullying Prussia – a view strongly backed by British public opinion.

The Queen, astonishingly, successfully intrigued with the Leader of the Opposition against her Prime Minister and even threatened to dissolve Parliament if she did not get her way. Her behaviour was most unconstitutional but she succeeded by obstinacy and determination. As late as 1880 she insisted 'she cannot and will not be the Queen of a democratic monarchy'.

Constitutional or not, of one thing she was sure – the British monarchy stood head and shoulders above all others in importance. Her eldest daughter became engaged to the Crown Prince of Prussia (the future Emperor of Germany, Frederick I). Victoria had been annoyed by the assumption in Prussia that the marriage would take place in Berlin, not London. This, she said, was 'too absurd . . . Whatever may be the usual practice of Prussian princes it is not every day that one marries the eldest daughter of the Queen of England!'

As she got older she became an object of veneration and she struck terror into everyone, even her own family. If they saw her walking towards them in the garden they would hide behind a bush or run in the opposite direction to avoid bumping into her. Even when grown up her children stood in so much awe of her that they were afraid to approach her directly and used her Private Secretary, Sir Frederick Ponsonby, instead. Every morning after breakfast members of the family waited in trepidation lest they receive one of her notes informing them of her displeasure about something or other the previous day and announcing the infliction of some punishment – e.g. withdrawing the use of horses.

She could also be inconsiderate to the point of cruelty. When visiting a library the librarian seized the opportunity to introduce his daughter. The Queen simply ignored him, said pointedly, 'I came to see the library' and swept onwards. Her tactlessness could be legendary. Her granddaughter, Princess Marie-Louise, recalled her telegraphing to her parents who were abroad, 'Children very well but poor little Louise very ugly.'

Wherever she happened to be everything revolved around Victoria, her whims and convenience. The Secretary of State for War, Sir Henry Campbell-Bannerman, staying for the first time at Balmoral, wrote to his wife – 'It is the funniest life conceivable – like a convent. We meet at meals and, when we are finished, each is off to his cell.' No one was allowed to leave the castle until the Queen had gone out – which was often not before 4 o'clock.

The rooms were chilly and draughty – Victoria believed that cold was healthy. Lord Redesdale once arrived at Balmoral when it was bitterly cold and snowing to discover the entire entourage had gone out on a picnic. To avoid freezing to death it was necessary to adopt cunning ruses. In 1896 Lord Salisbury, visiting Balmoral for talks with the Tsar, took the precaution of specifying that, on doctors' orders, the temperature of his room must be not less than 60 degrees.

Victoria abominated smoking – which was allowed only in a

small room austerely furnished like a guardroom with a wooden table and chairs. It was reached by going out of doors and crossing the kitchen courtyard. She looked on it as a kind of opium den. One government Minister was discovered flat on his back in his bedroom puffing cigar smoke up the chimney. She had a keen nose and told Ponsonby not to smoke when deciphering telegrams because the official box in which he sent her the papers smelt strongly of tobacco.

She always insisted on rigid formality. A visitor described his experience as 'rather a perpendicular evening' because palace life always involved a lot of standing around. The poet, Lord Tennyson noted, 'You must stand until the Queen asks you to sit down. But Her Majesty does not often tell you to sit down.' She had little sympathy for the physical strain of this excessive formality. When her physician once fell down, exhausted, in a faint after dinner she merely peered at him and complained sniffily, 'And a doctor too!'

Sitting down at table revealed other perils. She was a fast eater and all her life gobbled her food. Supper was timed to last exactly half an hour, with servants in knee breeches bringing soup, fish, cold sirloin of beef, sweet and dessert in rapid succession. Anyone who had failed to finish before the Queen, had his plate snatched away by a footman and the next course served.

The 8th Duke of Devonshire once caused scenes worthy of a Bateman cartoon. Dining one night at Windsor he was enjoying a saddle of four-year-old mutton – a speciality of the house. He paused in the midst of his conversation and suddenly realised that his barely touched dinner had vanished. Unprecedentedly he barked sharply at the footman, 'Here, bring that back!'

Forgetting the precedent of her distinguished ancestor, King Canute, Victoria expected even the weather to conform to her orders. On a sea-crossing to Ireland the Royal Yacht encountered rough weather. A huge wave caused her to lurch, almost knocking the Queen off her feet. She sent a message to the bridge: 'Give the admiral my compliments and tell him he's not to let that happen again.'

At the Diamond Jubilee service at St Paul's Cathedral in 1897 it was realised that a statue of Queen Anne would block the way of the procession and the view of the crowd. It was suggested to her that it be moved. She flatly refused to contemplate it. 'What a ridiculous idea! Move Queen Anne? Most certainly not. Why, it might some day be suggested that my statue should be moved, which I should much dislike.'

Sometimes Victoria could be cruelly unfair. In 1839 she suspected the unmarried Lady Flora Hastings of being pregnant, as her stomach appeared to be swelling rapidly. On hearing about the damaging rumours, Lady Flora subjected herself to a medical examination to prove her virtue intact. Infuriated by the unfairness of the scandal, her brother leaked the story to *The Times*, which whipped up public opinion on her behalf. Lord Melbourne prevailed on the Queen to visit her. But further doubts were put into her mind and Lady Flora continued to be ostracised virtually to her deathbed shortly afterwards. A post mortem then revealed the cause of the suspicious swelling – cancer of the liver. Her death inflamed hostility to the monarchy and court. The Queen was hissed in public – on one occasion by the Duchess of Montrose and Lady Sarah Ingestre. When they were identified Victoria replied 'Those two abominable women ought to be flogged.'

Victoria was frequently at odds with Prime Ministers throughout her reign – particularly Palmerston and Gladstone, who both served for long periods. Disraeli, however, found a key to success with her: 'Everyone likes flattery and when it comes to royalty you should lay it on with a trowel.' Another key was complaisance: 'I never refuse; I never contradict. I sometimes forget.'

Mrs Gladstone well understood the cause of Disraeli's success and advised her husband, 'do pet the Queen'. But he was quite hopeless at this. Victoria fumed, 'He speaks to me as though I were a public meeting.' He came to personify everything she disliked – particularly democracy and radical changes. His obstinacy and imperiousness of manner fully matched her own and he combined this with a complete inability to explain things in simple and attractive terms.

When criticised for trying to avoid appointing Gladstone in 1880 she retorted: 'The Queen does not in the least care, but rather wishes it should be known that she has the greatest possible disinclination to take this half-crazy and really in many ways ridiculous old man.' She was deeply shocked that Gladstone had made a morally crusading foreign policy the centrepiece of his Midlothian Election Campaign. She believed that all questions of foreign policy were the particular preserve of the monarch and the patrician governing class. Allowing the masses to have a say in such questions was 'unheard-of and the only excuse for it – that he is not quite sane.'

When General Gordon was murdered by dervishes in Khartoum in 1884 Victoria sent a telegram of rebuke to Gladstone for his failure to send a relieving force in time, as she had repeatedly urged. She did not bother to encode the message, which was handed to him by a station-master as he got off a train. Her action was astonishing – a modern equivalent might be Queen Elizabeth II publicly telling John Major 'I told you so!' when the pound was expelled from the ERM.

Victoria made Gladstone's life a real misery and he complained to Lord Rosebery, 'the Queen alone is enough to kill any man'. When he retired in 1894 he had been an MP for 63 years and, since his first Ministerial appointment in 1834, had held most high government offices, serving a record four terms as Prime Minister. For all this she gave him 'not one syllable of thanks for all his years of faithful and honourable service and the Queen's letter was so curt as to be almost insulting.' She did invite the Gladstones for a valedictory stay at Windsor, where he thought she might have presented her portrait or some such gift to Mrs Gladstone. But there was nothing – 'For I cannot reckon as anything what appeared to be a twopenny-halfpenny scrap, photographic or other, sent during the forenoon of our departure by the hand of a footman.'

One reason why she disliked Gladstone was that she was a strong imperialist, whereas Gladstone denounced the Zulu war of 1879, the Afghan war of 1880 and the first Boer war of 1881 as imperialist wars. This incensed her: 'If we are to maintain our position as a first-rate Power . . . we must with our Indian Empire and large colonies, be prepared for attacks and wars somewhere or other continually.'

Even in the face of military adversity she was dauntless. On Black

Week in the Boer war three British generals were defeated one after another in battle. She told the Prime Minister, 'Please understand that there is no one depressed in this house; we are not interested in the possibilities of defeat; they do not exist.'

Surprisingly, she had a keen sense of humour and, unless within the earshot of young, unmarried women, was quite prepared to tolerate a risqué story. During the course of a long life she became a woman of the world, but she was often naive. When she was being shown over Trinity College, Cambridge by the Master, Dr Whewell, she peered over the bridge across the river and asked innocently, 'What are those pieces of paper floating down there?' These were the days before the introduction of modern sewers. Whewell, demonstrating superb intellectual dexterity but little regard for truth, replied, 'Those, ma'am are notices saying that bathing is forbidden.' Again, when she was informed that Cecil Rhodes was a woman-hater she replied, 'Oh! I don't think that can be so. He was so civil to me.'

Victoria very much enjoyed the unexpectedly ludicrous. She once invited Admiral Foley to lunch to hear of the salvage of HMS *Eurydice*, a frigate sunk off Portsmouth. Having discussed the topic at length she then inquired after her friend, the admiral's sister. Somewhat hard of hearing, he thought she was still talking about the ship and replied, 'Ma'am I'm going to have her turned over, take a good look at her bottom and have it well scraped.' At this the Queen put down her knife and fork, hid her face in her handkerchief and laughed convulsively until the tears ran down her cheeks.

On another occasion the Duchess of Atholl recalled a comical advertisement which was published regarding the Dunkeld and Blairgowrie coach. The coach was called 'The Duchess of Atholl' and the inn from which it started was 'The Duke's Arms'. The notice informed the public that 'The Duchess of Atholl leaves the Duke's Arms every lawful morning at six o'clock.' The Queen roared with laughter.

Her public face was very different. She has come down to us as dour and humourless, largely because of one remark, 'We are not amused'. Viewed as a national institution rather than a human being, she personified not just the country but a whole age. When she died in 1901 the age died with her. Queen Victoria was a most formidable Battleaxe and, in the words of her son-in-law, the Duke of Argyll, 'she went down like a great three-decker ship'.

Janet Street-Porter

'I'm not interested in people who aren't brilliant. Can you imagine
the horror of going to dinner with people you don't know? They
could be really dreary! You'd end up being the entertainment,
wouldn't you?'
*****

Janet Street-Porter must enjoy a good soliloquy - in talking to
herself, at least she knows she'll be guaranteed some intelligent
conversation. But, she is no Greta Garbo and hates being alone.
Possibly she is concerned that, with no distractions, she might be
driven round the bend by the sound of her own voice.

She talks incessantly, her generous mouth relentlessly opening
and shutting, her overflowing brilliant-white goofy teeth flashing
brightly like a ship's semaphore. A lanky 6'1", her 'linguini legs' are
barely clad by a pelmet of microskirt. She spatters out f-words in an
exaggerated cockney accent – she is 'a Ba'leaxe an' naow mistike'.
She has a laugh like a chain-saw. She stands out in a crowd like a
combination of lighthouse and foghorn.

Clearly believing these characteristics insufficient to mark her out
from the herd, she also adopted fluorescent magenta hair, safety-
pin jewellery, big garish specs and a variety of arresting clothes.
Inspired by Diana, Princess of Wales, Janet recently rushed her own
exotic wardrobe of 65 flamboyant designer frocks to Christie's.
What her dresses lacked in femininity, they made up for in sheer
vulgarity and impact. A former TV (television not transvestite)

colleague commented: 'We consider that Janet has done for fashion what the M25 has done for hedgehogs.' Amazingly, the dresses proved less popular than those of the Princess of Wales; 11 lots failed to find a buyer, causing Christie's spokesman to comment, 'I think Janet Street Porter has a very individual personal style which possibly does not appeal to everyone.'

She has been likened to 'a horrible maladjusted teenager, swearing, scowling, slouching around'. Punctuality is the politeness of kings but Janet 'is always at least half an hour late for interviews and seems to make a point of NOT apologising'. One of her underlings, in the apparent belief that her rudeness is mitigated by being universal and not selective says, 'She grossly overcommits herself, is hugely disorganised and unreliable about time if you're not important.' Another critic describes her as someone who has never grown-up: 'a 25 year old trying to get out of the body of a 50 year old.'

Her father, Frank Bull, was a council electrician, her mother a school dinner lady; her sister still works on a Sainsbury's check-out till. Janet grew up in 1950s Fulham – in the days before gentrification, when working-class families occupied terraced houses which still had outside loos. In a patch of rough ground she was an exotic flower; viper's bugloss perhaps, 'a rather coarse border plant with showy summer flowers'.

When Janet was 14 her family moved up the A40 to respectable suburbia and Perivale. Janet went to a state girls' grammar school and emancipated herself from class limitations whilst retaining (indeed exaggerating) the vowels. Her extraordinary appearance belies a sharp brain. She was once in the local Young Conservative Quiz Team.

Told she would never get on in life unless she had elocution lessons, she taught herself even broader Cockney and became a Master of Whine (Middlesex nasal variety). Clever at school, she achieved 11 O levels and 4 A levels. Though obviously swotty, she achieved these results against a background of night-clubbing and dancing in the fleshpots of the West End, usually contriving to miss the last train home and disobeying her parents' feeble efforts to impose a curfew.

She went on to study at the Architectural Association School, but dropped out after a year 'because competition is the driving force in my life . . . and I could never be as good as Piers Gough, who sat next to me.' Gough has recently designed her futuristic house in the East End, half cottage – half castle. She left the AAS without a qualification but with a man – her first husband, Tim Street-Porter.

She was already engaged at the time but 'she was wild and wonderful' and Tim snatched her from under the nose of her fiancé to marry her in 1967. They gave up architecture and Janet began building a media career instead, firstly as a fashion writer. Moving into fashionable Limehouse, as neighbours of David and Debbie Owen, they bought a house and a billiard table.

In 1974 she left Tim but kept his surname. 'She can be quite devastating when she wants to be,' he said. Husband number two, Tony Elliott, ran *Time Out* magazine. He ran Tim out too. But, apparently the S-P split-up was quite amicable. Tony moved in on Janet, Tim moved into Tony's flat and Janet kept the billiard table.

Within a few months Tony's time was up and he was out too, with Janet citing Emma Soames in a divorce petition. Only a year or so later Janet was out of the revolving door again and into her third marriage – to Frank Cvitanovich, a Canadian film director 18 years her senior.

Husband No 3 introduced her to the Yorkshire Dales and fell-walking, two enthusiasms which endured though the marriage did not. In due course, Janet became an unlikely but effective President of the Ramblers' Association. However, Frank's penchant for straying off the beaten track was tested by another new enthusiasm of Janet's.

Dining at a London restaurant, he saw Janet stride in, dangling a toyboy from her arm like a Gucci handbag, at a time when she was supposed to be filming in Cumbria. Her escort was Tony James, a pint-sized bass player in a short-lived pop group. He was eight inches shorter and nine years her junior. She and the new Tony were to be seen for a while 'incongruously tramping across the Dales like a mother flamingo and her chick'.

Although Janet celebrated her third divorce in 1988, she did not have enough time to marry Tony before moving on to Normski – a frenetic black rapper and dancer, 20 years younger but her equal in height. She promoted him on one of her shows and he won the approval of husband No 1, Tim: 'He is a great character. They make a great couple. He talks as loudly as she does and is just as extrovert.' But, in time, the differences in age outweighed the similarities in the decibel count. Normski wasn't getting any younger. In 1995, he went the way of all male flesh – out.

In the search for eternal youth (though Janet's youths have been anything but), she married for the fourth time, 'quietly' in Las Vegas. David Sorkin, the then unemployed son of a north London lorry driver and 22 years her junior was the next holder of the title.

She once described her attitude to relationships as 'Like having this nice big pile of chips (gaming, not fish-and-). Bit by bit the chips go, the pile gets smaller till there's only a couple left, one of those goes and, well, it's time to move on . . . '

After jobs with *Petticoat*, the *Evening Standard* and the *Mirror*, and with her outsize talent for provocative and outlandish behaviour, it was a surprise when Janet half-joined the Establishment as Head of the Youth Department at the BBC. 'I soon figured out if you wannabe in charge, you gottabe runnin' television, not on it,' she explained.

Instantly christened (mimicking her cockney twang) 'The Yoof Department', it gave Janet control of a budget rising to £35 million a year, won her prizes and awards, and lots of stick from the press and colleagues who were jealous of her go-getting success and flamboyance.

Asked about her faults, she admitted, 'I'm not very good in queues at airports. My husband says I behave in an unpleasant queenly manner at check-in desks, causing us to have embarrassing spats as I try to throw my weight around to no avail.'

`Wimmin',' she says, 'have a built in bullshit-detector.' With such antennae, she is dismissive of TV male executives who 'sit at planning meetings as if they are re-writing the New Testament when it's only entertainment.'

A sunburst of Technicolor in the monochrome BBC, she towered above most of her media contemporaries and dismissed her male colleagues as a 'Masonic league of ritualistic men in grey suits' and

'Notta single one you coulda fancied.' After gaining accolades as the head of 'Yoof TV', the stuffed shirts passed her over for various jobs she had coveted – Head of Music and Arts, Controller of BBC2, Controller of BBC1. An ex-colleague explains: 'Janet was just too dangerous for the BBC . . . there are people who thought she was too vulgar to make it to the top.' In 1995 she walked out, after nine years, to join Mirror Group's new cable entertainment channel, *Live-TV*.

During her MacTaggart Memorial Lecture at the Edinburgh Television Festival in 1995 she castigated British TV management for being dominated by M-people – Male, Middle-class, Middle-brow, Middle-aged, Masonic and Mediocre. Unless things changed, she said, British TV would never be more than a bit-part player, forever doomed to be part of Rupert Murdoch's global theme park. She castigated Auntie Beeb as the 'Clark's shoes of multimedia; something which your Mum would buy for you but you'd never choose yourself.' British TV should emulate the British record industry, which exports nine times as much. Janet explains why – 'the TV industry is disadvantaged because it is better educated and more middle class.'

They could just about put up with being described as 'male and middle class' but calling the leaders of the mediacracy 'mediocre' was a declaration of war. Some of the 'suits', Armani or otherwise, tried to distance themselves from her barbs. 'I'm rather optimistically hoping that she didn't mean me,' wailed Alan Yentob, controller of BBC1. Others simply waited for her to fall into an elephant trap of her own making.

Sure enough, within weeks – in September 1995 – 'glad, confident morning' at *Live-TV* was over and Janet left her job as managing director after all of three months, following a widely reported rift between herself and Kelvin MacKenzie, Mirror Group TV's Head. They had never got on brilliantly. When MacKenzie was editor of the *Sun* he had printed an unflattering photograph of Janet alongside a picture of a horse, and invited readers to judge which was the more ugly.

When she offered him £1000 to find her a fourth husband Kelvin replied: 'With your looks, I'll accept it as a down-payment.'

When she announced she was going to see her osteopath, Kelvin suggested that Janet (racehorse-fit and looks 35) should go to a plastic surgeon instead. Janet replied breezily to the tubby, rumpled and balding MacKenzie, 'Hey Kelv, we're exactly the same age. Funny, innit?' He did not see the joke.

After her attack on the male culture of TV management, Kelvin took the blokeish decision, without telling Janet, to commit *Live-TV* to covering Rugby League matches – which he thought was entertainment but she did not. That was the straw that broke the camel's back.

Janet hates to be messed around. At the BBC, she stood no nonsense from temperamental reporters. To complaints she would reply, 'If you have problems with your job, I'm sure there are plenty of other people around who would like it.' Her philosophy was 'It's no good being nice to them. They hate you.' As she could not sack Kelvin she solved the problem at *Live-TV* by sacking herself.

Whilst no slouch at self-publicity, she has taken a lot of flak from men vastly less attractive and infinitely more boring. She dismisses their gibes – 'There are lotsa men around and I've never been without a boyfriend. Funny innit?' Their attacks rarely acknowledge her talent, her dynamism or her achievements.

She is scathing about 'the Suits' but no feminist stereotype. 'I think like a man. I suppose I'm a woman – I've got a pair of tits – but I don't believe in singling women out as a disabled group. I fight my own fights.' Temporarily out of the mainstream, she is a Battleaxe in search of a worthy battle.

Queen Mary

(b.1867 – d.1953)

'I am beginning to lose my memory but I mean to get it back.'

*****

In the epoch of 'It's a Royal Knockout' it is difficult quite to recapture the terrifying starchiness of autocratic royalty. But merely a glance at a photograph of Queen Mary in her later years will do the trick.

Standing upright with whaleboned stiffness, her neck covered with row after row of pearls in what appears to be, literally, a 'choker', her eyes set in a basilisk stare, Queen Mary was the epitome of the 'grande dame.' It would be *lèse majesté* to apply the term Battleaxe to her; it would also be inadequate to describe her true awesomeness.

In photographs she appears taller than her 5'6" because of her imposing deportment, enhanced by her long dresses, toque hats and shoe heels. Her standards were uncompromising and her manner imperious. She eschewed cosmetics and strongly disapproved of them in others. The Duchess of Westminster kissed the Queen's hand at a ball, leaving a scarlet lipstick imprint on Her Majesty's kid glove. The Duchess reminisced: 'She gave me one withering look that said all and I slunk away in disgrace.'

Although considerate by nature, the Queen was undemonstrative in affection and could freeze by a glance if offended.

Her private secretary's wife, Lady Ponsonby, referred to 'the cold egotism which seems to chill you in all royalties'.

Germanic in ancestry and betraying a slight guttural accent to the end of her life, she was nevertheless quintessentially English. Her father was an impoverished German, the Duke of Teck; her mother, Princess Mary of Cambridge, first cousin to Queen Victoria.

Queen Mary's father was only half royal, the product of a morganatic marriage. This meant, for genealogically pedantic German royals, that she lacked an acceptable pedigree and was obliged to find a suitable husband from Britain. Unfortunately, as her biographer observed, 'she was too royal to marry an ordinary English gentleman, and not royal enough to marry a Royalty'.

She was rescued from this marital limbo-land by the surprising unconventionality of Queen Victoria, who decided that she would make an excellent consort for her grandson, Prince Albert Victor, elder son of the future Edward VII. Various racy rumours circulated about the Prince – one that he frequented the notorious homosexual brothel in Cleveland Street; another that he was Jack the Ripper. Clearly, there was scope for a wife.

His father wrote to Queen Victoria: 'A good sensible wife with some considerable character is what he needs most.' Mary was just the person to sort him out and they were engaged on 3 December 1891. Her effect upon him must have been electric. On 7 January he felt unwell. Two days later he sank into delirium. By the 14th he was dead!

The investment in the abortive royal betrothal was not, however, wasted. In just over a year Mary was engaged to her dead fiancé's younger brother, Prince George. They married in July 1893 and received 1500 wedding presents valued at £300,000. Princess Mary, frugal by royal standards, chose a trousseau which included a mere 40 outdoor suits, fifteen ball gowns and innumerable bonnets, shoes and gloves.

In 1910 Prince George became King George V. After the glitter of the Edwardian Age dull domesticity descended upon Buckingham Palace. Instead of bridge after dinner and bohemianism in the bedroom, the King busied himself with his stamp collection whilst the Queen embroidered. They were both sticklers for order, duty and punctuality. By royal standards they were austere.

Queen Mary's parents had found it impossible to live on £10,000 a year in the 1870s (equivalent to millions today) and ran up debts from which they were obliged, from time to time, to flee abroad. Queen Mary, in contrast, became a martinet of frugality in a war against extravagance.

Her granddaughter, Queen Elizabeth II, told Hugh Gaitskell at a Downing Street dinner in the freezing winter of 1947 that Queen Mary's house was the coldest she knew, with hardly any fires anywhere. Gaitskell inquired whether this was because the Queen was spartan or the house naturally cold. He was told it was because Queen Mary considered it her national duty not to use fuel.

She introduced a revolutionary innovation into the royal dining room – the napkin ring. A clean napkin was no longer provided for every meal thus saving on laundry bills. Whilst staying with Lady Curzon in the country, the Queen's car ran over a stray lamb on the road. On her orders, it was immediately parcelled up and taken to the kitchens. For dessert, she once gave a startled clergyman lunching at Sandringham a half eaten pear from her plate!

Although parsimonious in expenditure she was predatory in her acquisitiveness. Pictures, furniture, objects of vertu captivated her interest, especially if they had royal associations. She was notorious, on visits to country houses, for making offers which could not be refused but which did not usually involve money.

Her first sally, upon sighting some desirable object, was to hint heavily, 'I am caressing it with my eyes.' Often, her reputation having gone before her, this would be sufficient to inspire the hapless host to part with it immediately. If not, the Queen would try again. On departure she might say archly: 'May I go back and say goodbye to that dear little cabinet?' If even that failed to disgorge the piece, she would follow up the visit with a brazen offer in writing to 'buy' it. The embarrassed recipient of the royal letter would then feel compelled to part with it as a gift.

Her imperiousness extended, also, to artistic scholarship. Her interest in art owed more to the historical and royal connections of the picture than to aesthetics. When she was told that a portrait group of Frederick, Prince of Wales, playing the cello to his sisters was by Philippe Mercier, not Joseph Nollekens, she replied 'We prefer the picture to remain as by Nollekens.'

The Queen's interest was narrow – family portraits and royal iconography. The King's interest in art was largely confined to postage stamps. His taste in pictures was even less advanced than Queen Mary's. Looking at a French Impressionist painting at the opening of the Tate Gallery extension, he shouted out to the Queen, 'Here's something to make you laugh, May.' Cézanne virtually inspired apoplexy – he was observed shaking his stick at one of his 'daubs' in the National Gallery. Turner fared no better. He told Sir Kenneth Clark, then its director, 'I tell you what, Turner was MAD. My grandmother (Queen Victoria) always said so.'

Just as Queen Mary's approach to art was extremely practical so was her approach to life. She once witnessed an apoplectic fit by General Sir Dighton Probyn VC, Treasurer to Queen Alexandra, and the great difficulty experienced in opening the tight collar of his uniform. In future, she always carried a sharp knife in her handbag, just in case of a similar need.

In September 1939 she was obliged to leave London for the duration of the war. This was 'not at all the thing', in her opinion, and she regarded it as a grave dereliction of duty. The King persuaded her, explaining that she would cause needless trouble and anxiety if she stayed behind. She arrived at Badminton House, the Gloucestershire seat of the Duke of Beaufort, accompanied by the majority of the 63 servants she maintained in London, together with their dependants.

She was not interested in country pursuits – had never learned to ride and knew nothing of the hunting field or farming. The Duchess of Beaufort conducted her around the estate and, pointing out to her a remarkable hayfield, elicited the equally remarkable royal response: 'So that's what hay looks like!'

As a septuagenarian in rural seclusion, she was unable to engage the enemy personally. However, listening to one of Hitler's speeches on the wireless, she roundly criticised his 'abominable' German. She bore the privations of war (including the loss of a son) with customary stoicism, and devoted herself to the continuation of a private war on ivy and unruly shrubs.

Her antipathy to ivy had been legendary at Sandringham and she devoted herself unilaterally and single-mindedly to its destruction. Her staff and, indeed, anyone staying in the house, would be pressed to serve in her 'Ivy Squad' formed to satisfy her basic instinct for tidiness and order by hacking down the hated creeper wherever it reared its head.

She busied herself in other war work – in particular the collection of 'salvage'. She noted in her diary for December 1939: 'Some Birmingham evacuee children came to help and we salvaged old bones, tins etc., evidently an old rubbish heap, while others cut down elders. I raked away a lot of rubbish.'

Her enthusiasm sometimes exceeded her understanding of the material. Several times she returned in her green Daimler heavily laden with what she thought to be scrap iron, but which was actually a field harrow or some other machinery left out in the fields in all weathers. These implements had to be discreetly returned to their owners without the Queen's knowledge.

Her attitude to night air-raids was phlegmatic. A reinforced room on Badminton's ground floor was used as a shelter. At first she descended there with the rest of the household. But whilst they might be discovered in the shelter at 3 a.m. dishevelled and half asleep in their dressing gowns, Queen Mary would be perfectly dressed, sitting bolt upright solving a cross-word puzzle. She soon decided to pay no attention whatever to the Luftwaffe and stopped 'descending'.

She was indomitable and battled to the end. Shortly before she died in March 1953 she announced: 'I am beginning to lose my memory but I mean to get it back!'

Claire Rayner

'I'm deeply practical; a stubborn old bag who won't be manipulated by editors.'

*****

Bulgarian pop-artist Christo has made a name for himself by wrapping up buildings like the Reichstag and calling the result a work of art. Seeing Claire Rayner clad in voluminous white shirt makes one wonder if she has been given the Christo treatment too. Of course, many women of her type and age are said to resemble public buildings. But she is more than that – she is a national institution.

One thing is certain. Nothing about Claire Rayner is under wraps except her imposing frame. Everything else hangs out – indeed is thrown out to envelop whoever is listening. And, even if you're not listening, you can't help hearing.

Claire Rayner is built to last. She seems unconvinced, however. Looking down upon her superstructure, making a sweeping gesture down her clothes and body she declares: 'All this will return to the earth and be eaten by worms and maggots. It's just part of the life-cycle, luvvie. If we're lucky enough to have children we might leave a few genes behind. Otherwise our only after-life is in the form of iron, water and sodium in the earth.'

It is difficult to believe that Claire will ever be reduced to her component elements. She is more of a cosmic life-force emitting energy like the sun, sweeping over, under and through whatever lies in its path.

She has an opinion on everything and everyone. Always ready to advise – even if you think you don't want advice, she'll advise you of the need to be advised. 'Motormouth' is one apt soubriquet to describe her relentless compulsion to talk and her mission to improve by getting everyone to see the world through her eyes.

This is not to everyone's taste: 'An irritating, jabbering omnipresence' was one commentator's opinion. And how about this: 'She is a horrendous personage. Peddling her vulgar brand of amoral humanism to simple-minded and ignorant mass audiences, including many suggestible children, must have done a hundred thousand times more harm to this country than an intelligent and civilised man like Richard Gott (*Guardian* journalist with links to the KGB) can ever have done by peddling his refined brand of middle-class fun-Marxism to small numbers of already long-converted *Guardian* readers.'

Claire Rayner is a household name – 'like Harpic,' she says helpfully. There are some who think that the famous advertisement for that toilet disinfectant accurately applies to her: 'clean round the bend'. Like her or loathe her, she has an impact. She was once described as 'more influential than the Archbishop of Canterbury when it comes to directing the nation's morals' (but that isn't saying much, these archiepiscopal days).

Now best known as the nation's favourite Agony Aunt, Claire Rayner was born Jewish in 1931. She grew up in considerable poverty in the East End and later in Canada. Her childhood was traumatic. She was unloved and unwanted. She describes her parents as 'awful people, barmy, potty, totally, utterly, hopelessly self-absorbed'. Her father was a 'feckless man, good for nothing much'.

As a child she could never keep still. She learned to read at three. At ten years old and 'smart as monkeys' (her words) she decided God did not exist and there was no after-life. Whether she advised God of this is not clear. Her life experience since childhood has made her 'deeply irreligious'. As a kid she was a red-hot Communist and wrote poems with deeply unpoetic titles like 'Proletariat Love'. Her doctrine is infallibility; her religion, common sense.

She was brought up to believe she was the ugly duckling – in contrast to her mother, who was very pretty. 'It's a terrible handicap being pretty. Personality is worth infinitely more. She's good and dead now. Well under. Best place for her.' If that shocks, bear in mind that her parents' treatment of her was shocking too.

Her parents emigrated to Canada after the war, leaving her behind in England. Later, they sent her a ticket to follow them, promising that life would be wonderful. When she got there she fell ill. An overactive thyroid gland produced hyperactivity, dramatic weight loss and popping eyes. Unfortunately, this was mis-diagnosed as hypomania and she was placed in a psychiatric hospital for 14 months.

Her only visitor in all that time was her sister. Her parents didn't visit once. On her release, her parents refused to pay her hospital bills. One of her grandparents had to bail her out. She returned to England and never saw either of her parents again.

Solid and comforting like a ship's figurehead, Claire's philosophy is based on the belief that 'a certain degree of toughness is needed in this rotten old world. Why should it be fun and roses all the time? Life is what matters. When you have been the butt of derision all your life a bit more doesn't bother you. Do the best with what you've got and let the rest go hang.

'I'm five foot nine and built like a bus. What can I do about it? Bugger all.' Life as a teenager was not easy: 'Five foot nine. Size 8 feet. Size 7 gloves. I could never stand up at parties. If a boy was chatting to me and I stood up he would probably have fainted.'

She is married to pony-tailed painter, Desmond. She had 'fancied him something rotten' and wanted to live in sin, perhaps as a reaction to her parents. But he insisted she made an honest man of him. Claire is now the mother of three grown-up children.

She likes to shock, but in a motherly way. She once demonstrated how to use a condom on early morning TV. 'What's outrageous about that, darling? It is education.'

Defensive about being known only as an Agony Aunt, Claire writes novels (around 50 to date) and earns a fortune from them. Literary Editors are sniffy about her, and she may not get reviews, but the books sell. Lack of critical esteem doesn't bother her. Like

Liberace, she cries all the way to the bank.

'The Rayners Live Here' booms the plaque on their huge North London house. The indoor swimming pool ('the best toy I ever had') was built with money from her book *Maddie*. She wrote it after seeing the Greek tragedy *Medea*. Like Medea, Maddie kills her children and Claire savours the delicious irony that the book was featured in a Mother's Day promotion by the Publishers' Association. 'They can't have read it. Utter bliss!'

A serial talker, Claire leaves interviewers floundering in her wake, calling them 'darling', 'luvvie' and 'ducks'. Statuesque and forthright in her views, she is never afraid to speak her mind. She wants us to do away with music in shops, shopping malls, miniskirts, lavatory deodorants and Ken and Barbie dolls; they are repulsive. Things that ought to be brought back: trams, the proper taste of baked beans, eel pie and mash shops, whips and tops.

She is a communicator and deeply distrusts scientists and other 'experts' who refuse to bring themselves down to the level of ordinary folk. 'How on earth are you going to persuade ordinary people if you speak a private language we cannot understand?'

She articulates the views of middle England, especially women. She rails against men who do not use deodorants, especially in heat waves. 'It's been perfectly disgusting to be out and about during these dog days. When will it dawn on them that the rich, manly effluent they find so tolerable in themselves means a severe olfactory overload for the rest of us. Trying not to inhale in the presence of men does it for me.

'I'm deeply practical; a stubborn old bag who won't be manipulated by editors.' She tried not to be manipulated either by Dr Anthony Clare when he interviewed for *In The Psychiatrist's Chair*. She managed to avoid many of his more penetrating questions about her childhood. But the armour-plating was pierced and her remorseless cheeriness turned to sobs as she described the physical and emotional bullying she suffered at the hands of her parents.

Her extrovert personality seems to be a reaction to those dreadful experiences of childhood which lie consciously suppressed almost all the time. Claire's enormous laugh cheers the soul. Declaring chocolates evil and villainous she says that counting calories is deeply silly and sad. 'I'm awfully glad I didn't discover anorexia. We don't all have to look as if we came out of the same tube of toothpaste.' But, somewhat wistfully, she has admitted it would have been nice to go through life little. 'Slender as the morning, lovely as the dawn'.

If she had, the world's decibel count would probably have been much lower. Big, blowzy, breathy and bossy, Claire Rayner is an archetypal Battleaxe – she had real battles to fight in her dysfunctional upbringing. The kind of love and support which her parents failed to give, brims over in her and impels her to fight life's battles for those too weak or clueless to fight for themselves.

Dame Irene Ward

(b. c.1895 – d.1980)

'What absolute bosh you are talking' (To Adolf Hitler)
*****

In the darkest days of the Second World War there was a serious shortage of blue serge, the material used for making naval uniforms. A choice had to be made. Should the limited supplies be earmarked for the men at sea on battle stations or for the WRNS serving ashore? The Admiralty decided the fighting men should take priority.

Questions were asked in the House. Dame Irene Ward, the redoubtable Conservative MP for Tynemouth, rose in her place. This, in itself, was an awesome sight – Dame Irene was more a Battleship than a Battleaxe.

She fired off a salvo at the hapless First Lord of the Admiralty: 'Is the Minister telling me that the skirts of the Wrens must be held up until the needs of the Navy have been satisfied?'

The House collapsed with mirth, greatly enhanced by the obvious innocence with which the question was asked.

Dame Irene came from a more innocent age – an age when Tory ladies wore hats. The ladies on the platform at a Conservative Party Conference, even up to the 1970s, positively bristled with hats. The sight of all those formidable females, many broad of beam, resembled nothing less than the British Battle Fleet riding at anchor in Scapa Flow. In her day Dame Irene was the flagship.

She first made an assault on a constituency in the north-eastern coal mining area of Morpeth in 1924. She lost then, and again in 1929, but won at Wallsend in 1931 which she held until the Labour landslide of 1945. She switched to the next door seat of Tynemouth in 1951 and held that until she retired in 1974. She then went into dry dock (but was certainly never mothballed) in the House of Lords as Baroness Ward of North Tyneside. She died in 1980.

She was possibly the most formidable woman ever to occupy the Conservative backbenches. She was born long before women were given the vote – exactly when remained a mystery as she never revealed her age to reference books. When first elected in 1931, she defeated Britain's first woman Cabinet Minister, Margaret Bondfield, to become one of only 13 women MPs.

A newspaper report of the time described her as having 'an adventurous disposition. A while ago she heard that efforts were to be made to raise the wreck of a famous vessel laden with gold from the depths of the sea. She was so intrigued that she wanted to be allowed to go down with one of the divers and, in order to become efficient in diving she visited a diving apparatus firm, donned a diving suit and practised in their tank.'

She quickly made her mark as a major House of Commons 'character'. She was a fearless defender of her constituency and every individual constituent. In a stuffier age she adopted unconventional methods of drawing attention to grievances.

On one occasion in 1960 she invaded the seat of the Leader of the House of Commons on the government front bench. Depositing her ironclad handbag on the seat adjoining the Prime Minister's, she refused to budge all through Question Time in order to draw attention to the plight of service widows on low pensions. She sat serenely and impassively, surmounted by an enormous fur hat, monopolising the attentions of the Press Gallery whilst Edward Heath struggled to answer questions from the Dispatch Box, affecting not to notice the indomitable Dame's unmistakable and mountainous presence.

Dame Irene's demonstration occurred many years before the student protests of the late 1960s made sit-ins fashionable. Her appetite was whetted by the success of this ploy in grabbing the headlines for another cause dear to her heart. She gained a reputation as a geriatric delinquent, and was once suspended from the House for blocking a Commons vote.

It all began quietly enough. Dame Irene, the political equivalent of Margaret Rutherford, silently steamed over the horizon into the Chamber wearing an impressive hat and a white gardenia. She manoeuvred herself into position and stood stolidly in front of the table which bears the mace and divides the two front benches. And there she stayed, and stayed, blocking the floor with her bulk, preventing the House from proceeding with its business, refusing to sit down and shouting protests at the Speaker.

Eventually, patience exhausted, the Speaker 'named' Dame Irene. MPs are normally referred to by their constituencies as 'the Hon. Member for . . .' but, in cases of very bad behaviour, the Speaker mentions the Member by name, which leads to his or her suspension from the House. This is usually accompanied by wild scenes of confusion and frequently by mirth.

To the delight of tourists in the Gallery, the Serjeant at Arms then moves forward to escort the miscreant Member from the Chamber. The Serjeant at that time was the equally redoubtable Rear Admiral Sir Alexander Gordon-Lennox, red-faced and well-fed, resplendent in velvet knee-breeches, black silk stockings and silver-buckled shoes. The Admiral inched forward with trepidation, his sword clanking from his waist. Used to engaging men o' war, his previous naval training had left him wholly unprepared for a broadside from this 'woman o' war'.

Dame Irene quivered with anger and waited until he berthed alongside her. He tapped her arm. She bowed to the Speaker, turned and bowed to the Tories and, stately as a galleon, started walking majestically towards the door. She brought the roof down by asking the Serjeant in a plainly audible stage whisper 'Will you take my right arm or my left?' as they swept out through a storm of cheers and laughter.

By reducing the proceedings to farce Dame Irene was actually making a serious point – that the government was curtailing discussion of the Budget and acting dictatorially.

She stood out amongst the greyness of what was then almost exclusively a male club. There was no more magnificent sight than Dame Irene, in the words of one commentator, 'rising flower-bedecked like Venus from a sea of handbags and papers to pose a question'.

Fiercely loyal to her own constituency she was not to be fobbed off by Ministers. Complaining that her Question about the shortage of hospital beds in her area had not been answered, the Speaker informed her that it had been minutes earlier, together with a broadly similar one about Cardiff. That was not good enough for Dame Irene. 'The Minister is a dictator. I do not like dictators. Why should Newcastle be done out of a reply. It is absolute nonsense.' The Minister sat silent while the battle raged between Dame Irene and the Speaker who tried to silence her with history, 'I think it was in 1693 this House first resolved that Members who are not speaking should keep quiet.' Dame Irene retorted, 'I was not born in 1693.' And that was that.

She always managed to have the last word, as in this exchange with the Secretary of State for War in 1943:

Dame Irene rose to her feet: 'Why are soldiers not allowed to use free travel vouchers to visit Luxor (near Cairo) like members of the RAF?' Sir James Grigg, 'You are misinformed. Free vouchers are granted to the nearest leave centre as in the RAF.' Dame Irene protested, 'That was not so when I was there.' Sir James; 'This isn't the first time I have had a dispute with you on a question of fact.' Dame Irene shot back; 'And it isn't the first time that I am right and you are wrong.'

She positively relished controversy and plain speaking and was unafraid to tackle anyone. She took part in a parliamentary delegation to Nazi Germany in 1936. During a diplomatic tea party at Ribbentrop's villa there was a sudden pause in the polite chatter and Dame Irene's stentorian voice could be plainly heard telling the Führer, 'What absolute bosh you are talking!'

Jean Rook
(b.1931 – d.1991)

'Watch out! She used to eat editors for breakfast.'
*****

'You could hear the clink and clatter of her rings and bracelets from 200 yards and that meant "Watch Out!" She used to eat editors for breakfast,' fondly recalled former *News of the World* editor, Derek Jameson.

Obituarised as 'Britain's bitchiest, best-known, loved and loathed woman journalist', Jean Rook's trenchant views and the brash, opinionated vulgarity in which she luxuriated, made her the greatest female name in tabloid journalism of her time.

She invented a type of column now as much a hallmark of our daily papers as the crossword – calculatedly abrasive in the style of the 'female columnist from Hell' satirised in *Private Eye*'s lampoon, Glenda Slag. Literature it definitely ain't!

Jean swore she never read Glenda Slag 'because it was too near the mark'. She feared some of the style might rub off on her and she would become the copy of Glenda rather than the reverse.

Fleet Street editors regarded her as that rarest of birds – a genuine circulation-puller in her own right, with a loyal phalanx of readers who would follow her if she moved to another paper. Her strength lay in the belief of tabloid editors that 'nobody ever lost money underestimating the public taste'. However, she did have standards. She may have been vulgar but she was not gross.

Jean Rook was often thought to have crowned herself as 'First Lady of Fleet Street'. In fact, the title was bestowed by an enthusiastic Deputy Editor at the *Daily Express* who heralded her arrival at the paper with the banner headline: 'She's Frank, Forthright, Formidable, Fearless and Infuriating. She is the First Lady of Fleet Street. You cannot afford to miss her!!!'

Tall and striking, with a mane of honey-blonde hair, frequently swathed in furs, wearing always a bold, confident brassy look, with swags of chunky gold jewellery, she swept majestically round the old *Express* building in Fleet Street (affectionately known in *Private Eye* as the Black Lubyanka) and never really came to terms with the move to the modern block across Blackfriars Bridge. 'A serial smoker, she was also addicted to the smell of printer's ink and the roar of the old-fashioned pre-computerised presses rolling the copy on its way.'

Loud, mocking and bitchy, her acid tongue articulated for millions. She was like an alley cat claiming a natural right to look askance at a king. Her questions were journalistically sharp because they were blunt: 'Take Jackie Onassis. What people want to know is – why does she have a daughter so bloody plain when she herself is so beautiful; or, did she know her husband was having affairs all over the place; and who she will marry next . . .'

She wrote in her autobiography *The Cowardly Lioness*, 'All Yorkshire people call a spade a shovel and, when roused, dig the graves of people who irritate them.' Jean feared nothing and, as if to prove it, she was the first journalist to enter the cage of a man-eating Bengal tiger – it never recovered from the shock.

Born in Hull, she was a stage Yorkshirewoman for whom plain-speaking was almost an act of religious observance. She never actually said 'I come from Yorkshire, where the weak die young and the strong envy them their fate' – but she might have done.

She inherited from her father an unassailable sense of self-worth and she attributed her volatility to him. She also never wavered from her mother Freda's urging to 'Stick to your guns if you think you're right'. Her mother later confirmed 'she hasn't a nervous bone in her body. Nobody would deter Jean' – except, possibly, Freda herself!

When Jean discovered she had breast cancer, she was convinced she was going to die any minute. Freda could not be doing with self-pity: 'Look. If you're so sure you're going to die, why don't you do it now and put yourself and the rest of us out of our misery? If you reach your eighties, aren't you going to feel a bloody fool looking at the wall and still thinking you're going to die.'

Mother's Yorkshire grit was mixed with shafts of grim humour. Jean's father was rarely rude but once, in exasperation, told Freda 'Oh, go to Hell!' Without a second's pause she shot back: 'Any message?' Jean inherited all these parental characteristics and displayed them in her writings.

Narrowly missing a First in English Literature at London University, she went on to study for an MA. Her thesis 'The Influence of T. S. Eliot on the English Drama of his Time' failed to impress the News Editor of the *Hull Daily Mail*, where she sought a vacation job: 'You have spent far too much time in education and I can tell you now, you haven't a cat in hell's chance of getting to Fleet Street.'

She began humbly enough as a graduate trainee on the *Sheffield Telegraph*, where she suffered at the hands of the News Editor, known familiarly as the Barnsley Bull. She had better luck at the hands of his Deputy, Geoffrey Nash, whom she went on to marry. Jean moved on to become Women's Editor of the *Yorkshire Post*, and then clawed her way up Fleet Street via the *Sun*, *Daily Sketch*, and *Daily Mail*, finally being lured to the *Daily Express* in 1972.

Attracted by a somewhat over-glamorous photograph of her, John Junor (then Editor of the *Sunday Express*) invited her to lunch with a view to poaching her from the *Daily Mail*. When he saw the brash, brassy reality he passed on the idea to the editor of his sister paper, the *Daily Express*. The *Mail*, from Lord Rothermere downwards, rightly believing her to be a major circulation booster, frantically tried to persuade her to stay – offering more money, more fringe benefits, more anything. But, having given her word to the *Express* she would not break it.

She enjoyed by far the biggest by-line amongst women journalists and, probably, the largest salary – supplemented by a Jaguar XJ6 resplendent with doeskin leather seats and walnut dashboard.

Despite being one of the brightest stars in the London's journalistic firmament, she kept her Yorkshire feet firmly planted on the ground and in touch with ordinary folk. People related to her because 'I am as ordinary as they are. I am the most ordinary person breathing.'

Her column was deeply personal and she attributed its success to writing about what people wanted to know. Jean Rook saw her role as representing the public mood, even though its swings often led to her treating public figures with wild schizophrenia, being adulatory one week, vitriolic the next.

She shared her life with the extended family of readers of her pithy, pun-laden column, once described as 'an excruciatingly alliterative mixture of mangled metaphors.'

Whilst a staunch supporter of the monarchy, she claimed hers was 'the first foot on the road to realistic reporting about the Royals'. Her Majesty the Queen must have been appropriately grateful for her advice on grooming – especially that the Royal eyebrows needed plucking.

The Duke of Edinburgh probably valued rather less her opinion of him as a 'bloody-minded man with a temper as foul as an arthritic corgi . . . an ill-mannered Greek immigrant who's been well paid by Britain for 42 years for doing nothing but put it down . . . a pompous, cantankerous, not obviously gifted foreign princeling . . . '

The Duchess of York became a frequent target. She proclaimed 'Fergie is a frump' and re-christened her the 'Duchess of Pork'. On another occasion she was 'like an unbrushed red setter struggling to get out of a potato sack'. She did temper this rancorous abuse with the concession that she was 'great fun, powerfully sexy, tremendously boisterous and thrilling to men'. Her husband, Prince Andrew, was less fortunate. She castigated his taste as 'about as subtle as a sat-on whoopee cushion'. Prince Edward was 'unready, unsteady, unemployed Eddie'.

Nor was there any Christian charity for the Archbishop of Canterbury, Robert Runcie, whom she dismissed as a 'silly, ineffectual old bleater we can do without'. Elizabeth Taylor did not escape either; 'as squat bottomed and broad beamed as an overpainted Russian doll'.

She was never more delighted than when a provocative piece produced an avalanche of letters, even if largely hostile. When she attacked Mary Whitehouse as 'a whited sepulchre who hands out black marks to programmes she doesn't watch', she received 1,000 letters within 48 hours, all but six wanting her sacked. 'That was super,' she said, 'it got me a big pay rise!'

(How many young journalists today would have any idea what a 'whited sepulchre' was? When my husband issued a press release in the last election applying this description to his principal opponent, we were besieged by reporters asking for a translation.)

Jean was as perceptive as she was abrasive. She claimed to be the first to spot Margaret Thatcher as Britain's first woman Prime Minister – in 1974, when she was only Education Secretary: 'She only looks like an angel cake. In fact she is a very well-baked rock bun.' There was a natural bond between Jean and Margaret Thatcher.

People crossed her at their peril not hers. When Sir Larry Lamb became Editor of the *Daily Express* he decided he did not want any stars of the show apart from himself and resolved to dispense with Jean. Staff compared the ensuing conflict to that between the Greeks and the Amazons, and held their breath as the battle raged back and forth behind closed doors. Jean needed no protection against a mere Editor (she survived eight at the *Express*) and emerged triumphant. She recorded subsequently that she bore three scars – her Caesarean, her lumpectomy and Larry Lamb.

Her latter years were very sad. In 1985 at their Kent home, she and Geoff suffered a terrifying ordeal. They were invaded by burglars who assaulted them, tied them up and ransacked the house, taking most of their silver and her jewellery. Jean wrote about it the next week in characteristically gutsy style. But, she and her husband never really recovered from the shock. He became ill and died of a brain tumour on their 25th wedding anniversary in 1988.

Jean herself died aged only 59 in 1991 after a two-year battle against breast cancer. She missed her deadline only twice in 20 years, once when she gave birth to her son Gresby, and secondly, when her cancer was diagnosed. Typically, after her son's birth she wrote the next column from hospital with her right hand, whilst she bottle-fed her son with her left. She said 'if he has ink in his veins it's probably literal'. Following the cancer diagnosis she devoted the column to her feelings on receipt of the awful news.

When she died the tributes were manifold. Margaret Thatcher said 'her incisive style, pithy comment and human insight livened the *Express* every time she wrote. Personally, she was very kind and understanding.'

She was warmhearted, kind and generous. She was a bit of a bogus Battleaxe. Much of her public façade was just that, a façade, and the woman behind it would always be the first to comfort, console and help others. Love her or hate her, most people admired her chutzpah and, in particular, the bravery she displayed fighting her cancer. She wrote about it very movingly, giving hope and inspiration to millions.

Teresa Gorman

*'You don't have to agree with me or even like me but you can't deny,
given my age, I'm still functioning on all cylinders and making
some kind of contribution.'*

*****

'Teresa is too cuddly and flirtatious to be a Battleaxe.' So says my
husband, Neil. But he is wrong! She certainly does not conform to
the conventional picture of the domineering, pushy Battleaxe,
unlike a few women MPs I could mention. But Teresa has battled as
indomitably as any Battleaxe for her ideas.

She married Jim when she was just 19. 'If I feel down (difficult to
imagine!) I just go home for a cuddle' she explains. During all-night
sittings at the Commons when she was not allowed to go home,
Neil provided the cuddles for two years; as Teresa's Whip, he was
responsible for making sure she stayed to vote.

An uncompromising individualist and libertarian, she believes
the State is part of the problem, not the answer. Her personal
philosophy is 'Mind your Own Business' and that we 'all have to go
to Hell in our own way'. At the bottom of her writing paper she has
an aphorism of Frederic Bastiat: 'The State is the great fiction where
everyone tries to live at the expense of everyone else.'

Bastiat was a French nineteenth century pamphleteer, who had
the unusual distinction of making free market economics amusing!
His satires exposing the fallacies of State intervention included the
'Petition of Candlemakers against the Sun, for competing unfairly

with their industry'. Every Brussels bureaucrat (particularly French technocrats) should be given a copy of his 'Economic Sophisms' and examined on it before being allowed to interfere with our lives.

Teresa's two pet hates are bureaucracy and Europe (seems like the same thing really). Having developed a successful independent business, she is allergic to mountains of forms, completed in triplicate and uselessly filed for eternity by faceless officialdom. She is a Battleaxe against Bureaucracy and the Nanny State.

Teresa was brought up in Putney and went to the local grammar school. 'I was cheeky then. Most of my education happened in the corridor outside the Head's study' – akin to the *Who's Who* entry of Sir Osbert Sitwell who boasted; 'Educated: in the holidays from Eton.' Although brainy, she was not encouraged to stay at school and left at 16.' After a succession of office jobs she put herself through teacher training college (her father wouldn't fill in a grant form to take money from the State). She emerged to teach biology but ten years of teaching did not fulfil, so she hopped off and obtained a First in zoology and botany from London University.

A spell in America opened her eyes to the potential of free markets and a deregulated society. 'America changed my life . . . it was like coming out from behind the Iron Curtain. Profit and success was a cause for celebration not envy and suspicion.' Back in Britain she and Jim started a successful small business supplying science teaching aids to schools and the Third World.

Her first foray into politics came in 1973, marching up and down outside the Palace of Westminster, waving a home-made placard with her slogan 'VAT kills. Kill VAT.' She had been moved to action after a small businessman committed suicide when hounded by the VAT man.

Her appetite whetted by protest outside the House of Commons, she tried to get inside. In the General Election of October 1974, she stood as an anti-Heath Independent candidate in Streatham. She was more concerned about her image then: 'I was worried the neighbours would think I was barmy so I stood in my maiden name.' She paid her deposit in gold Krugerrands to make the point that our paper money had become worthless because of Government-sponsored inflation. The grand total of 210 far-sighted electors voted for her and, within months, Heath was replaced by Margaret Thatcher.

Placards apart, she first made a political name for herself as a Westminster City Councillor when she called for the privatisation of the public loos. Teresa realised the public's convenience could be enhanced with soft lighting, soft paper, sweet music, comfortable seats, video-conferencing . . . and much else. If Teresa had bought them, she might have expanded the business into the nation's largest lavatory chain. Predictably she met deep-seated opposition – the cistern was against her. (That's enough pun-ishment, this is a serious book – Ed.)

She turned her attentions to another kind of safe seat – the parliamentary sort. Success was elusive to start with – 'Twelve times I was passed over in favour of inferior men, usually pimply youths'. She cheerfully admits she then told a slight terminological inexactitude to get selected for Billericay – she took ten years off her age. This was not quite the deception it appears, as she looks a good twenty years younger than anyone else born in 1931.

She is a doughty fighter for women at all levels. 'Women are industrious, inventive, patient, multi-talented and adaptable.' Men, however, are dismissed as 'status and demarcation-conscious'. She says she did not come into politics to work for women but, when she got there, realised 'no one was looking at things from the woman's point of view'.

'I have no time for people who blame all the world's trouble on single mothers. No woman ever became a single mother on her own.' Attacking a Euro-grant designed to get prostitutes off the streets and back into society, she declared, 'I don't know why these people should think prostitutes in Vienna and Bilbao want to improve themselves. That implies they are a lot of dummies who need improving.'

Teresa does believe in one literal and bloody use of the battle-axe – castration for rapists. 'If I had my way, I'd teach every schoolgirl to go for the groin in the event of an attack.' She is fed up with 'geriatric judges giving soft sentences to rapists. Most women would rather they cut off their goolies.' That remark earned her a place in the *Dictionary of Sex Quotations* under 'G' for 'goolies' – an entry of which she is ebulliently proud. She is generally thought to be possessed of more 'goolies' than most of her male colleagues in the House combined.

She describes the attitude of the Tory Party towards women as 'almost Edwardian – they are not friendly towards women – not if they grow old, which they think is a crime.' Fortunately, due to Hormone Replacement Therapy, Teresa has been getting younger as she gets older.

In the early years, she was ridiculed for her very vocal espousal of HRT. Adamant as ever, she set up the Amarant Trust in 1986 to 'put the menopause on the map' and raise money for research. Derided as 'Mrs Monkey Glands', she hit back: 'If men's testicles packed up at 50 you can bet your boots there would be treatment available.'

No one can possibly disagree with either that or the following remark, 'You don't have to approve of me or even like me, but you can't deny, given my age, I'm still functioning on all cylinders and making some kind of contribution.' – just like the Queen, the Queen Mother and Lady Thatcher, all of whom are rumoured to be taking the tablets.

She has a tendency to get into what she calls 'little scrapes'. Establishment figures use other words – like betrayal, disloyalty and back-stabbing. With a little help from a few high-principled colleagues, she has caused more trouble for the Party high-ups than most other backbenchers put together. Teresa takes it all in her bouncy stride, cheerfully announcing, 'It's not new to me to find myself in a situation where I appear to be swimming upstream.'

Opinionated and unafraid of upsetting people if necessary, she is dismissive of the 'wets' in her own Party: 'They are always caring for everyone all the time, these old style Tory patricians. They think they are born to rule . . . they ought to get out of people's way. I daresay some of the Tory old guard think I am quite frightful – a common, vulgar little woman, and an upstart from nowhere.'

She proudly supported John Redwood's leadership bid against John Major in 1995 but became disillusioned. 'As soon as he got a bit of flak because Euro rebels like me were backing him, his team made it clear we were bad news. I call that ill-mannered. He could have told the Press that we stood up for real Conservative values while they were pushing policies through Cabinet that most of us didn't believe in.'

John Major secured a rare plaudit from her in May 1996 when he was bullish about the beef crisis and threatened to block moves towards the European single currency. 'I don't know whether the PM is on Ecstasy or whether he had oysters for lunch, but he sure made an impact.' Less kindly, she once described him as 'looking like the leaning tower of pizza'.

Teresa's colours on Europe were firmly nailed to the mast, whilst the Major government hammered theirs to the fence. Long a thorn in the side of the Party hierarchy, she fought tooth and nail against the Maastricht Bill and resisted all the 'dirty tricks and double dealing' of the Tory Whips. She was one of the nine most persistent rebels who had the Tory Whip withdrawn, with veiled threats that a whipless MP soon becomes a constituency-less MP. Describing the loss of the Whip as 'very liberating', Teresa continued her implacable opposition to the Euro-nonsense, putting loyalty to her views and her country beyond loyalty to the regime.

In a post-interview chat with ITN's Michael Brunson, John Major incautiously described the rebels as 'bastards'. Unfortunately for him this was inadvertently recorded and, of course, leaked. He got into similar trouble by confiding that the name of Sir Richard Body (one of the most intransigent anti-EC rebels) reminded him of 'the flapping of white coats'. Sir Richard was not amused and resigned the Whip, causing Major to backtrack, but without success. Teresa, proud of her new illegitimacy, subsequently published a sprightly little book called The Bastards, cataloguing the inside story of the Whips' dirty tricks.

Neil, as Teresa's Whip, was given the task of trying to persuade her to vote with the Government when it sought approval of the Maastricht agreement in 1992. She ostentatiously sat out the Division in the Chamber while his cajolings went unheeded. He only had eight minutes before the doors were locked. He did his best to grapple with her but to no avail. The Speaker cried 'Lock the doors'. Taking off like a Saturn rocket, he reached the door just as the doorkeeper turned the key. Too late! He had involuntarily abstained along with Teresa!

When she does want to co-operate with the government, but not actually vote, she finds out if her 'pair' (Labour MP George Galloway) is voting by serenading him on the telephone, to the tune of an old Elvis favourite, 'Are you Voting tonight?'

In the early days she and Edwina Currie were often compared with each other. Whilst they are both strong Tory women, they have diametrically opposed outlooks on the world. Teresa has no time for the bossy paternalism espoused by Mrs Currie. Relations hit rock-bottom when the latter said in her second bonkbuster novel 'Teresa Gorman has at last succumbed to advancing years, stopped taking the tablets and shrunk to a benign little granny.' The idea of Teresa ever becoming benign, even if she lives to 110, is nonsense. She dismissed Edwina's tales of sex and sin in the shadow of Big Ben as, 'a triumph of imagination over experience . . . Edwina is no Disraeli.' The two had crossed swords many times, not least when Teresa published a book which did a convincing demolition job on Edwina's salmonella in eggs scare. Teresa, as a biologist, knew what she was talking about whilst Edwina did for the British poultry industry what Genghis Khan did for international diplomacy.

Her methods of dealing with difficult men are distinctly un-Battleaxey. She explained to Gloria Hunniford 'If he's 6ft 3in and looking down at me with a disdainful air while I'm making an important political point, I reach up and touch him on the nose. It always works.'

Teresa has no compunction about taking on the bureaucrats personally. She lives in Old Hall Farm, a 15th century Grade II listed house thought to have been built as an Essex residence for the Bishop of London. In 1993 she collided head-on with Thurrock Borough Council over some 'unauthorised alterations' she and Jim had made. She robustly dismissed the Council as 'a bunch of old Stalinists gunning for a Tory scalp', accusing them of 'malicious vindictive persecution'. The Council cheekily accused her of 'history replacement therapy' and said she had committed 33 breaches of listed building legislation. The fine for each offence could be £20,000, (not to mention several months in prison) so Teresa's solicitor earned his corn by persuading the Judge to consolidate them into a single offence, dramatically reducing the potential liability.

The Council sniffily described the improvements as 'tasteless pastiche', particularly a porch which was 'completely unacceptable, with no historical basis or stylistic relevance'. Absurdly, they also wanted to restore a window which had been inserted in Victorian times into the 15th century brickwork, which clearly had no historical basis or stylistic relevance to what was there originally. Presumably they would have forced her to brick it up if they had been around to enforce listed building controls 100 years ago!

Teresa launched a counter-offensive against the Council, inviting a phalanx of press and camera crews to see for themselves how she and Jim had transformed a derelict wreck into 'a little miracle'. After an impromptu press conference outside, she marched them around the property like a Japanese tourist guide with umbrella aloft, pointing out in particular a small grave and pet's tombstone in the garden. 'That,' she declared triumphantly, 'is the last Chief Planning Officer.'

She lost her legal battle and the Council forced her 'to right the wrongs'. Neil suggested that she put the porch on wheels, so that it could stay where it was but be moved at will, which would get around the legal problem and cause the petty bureaucrats to tear their hair out in frustration! Unfortunately, she has not so far adopted this highly practical solution.

She is unafraid of espousing unpopular causes in a fight against injustice. In 1988 she supported the Wimbledon ticket touts and commended their enterprise for 'providing a service'. 'Good luck to the touts. Their vulgar trade makes a £20 ticket worth £800 and I can see no criticism in what they are doing.' She castigated the organisers of Wimbledon for their 'upper class twittishness' and for running the championships 'like an Edwardian garden party'. The Chairman of the All-England Lawn Tennis Club, 'Buzzer' Hadingham, was 'a dear old Edwardian in aspic'.

A *Times* profile said 'By Westminster standards, she is something of an intellectual but, although highly educated, she expresses herself in the argot of *Carry On* films.' Favourite expressions include: 'absolute codswallop', 'tommyrot', and 'fiddlesticks'.

Described as 'a small bustling bundle of dynamism, given to occasional malapropisms', she is excellent and entertaining company. Funny and irreverent, she positively fizzes with bolshy individualism. Always dressed in bright colours, frequently canary yellow or lime green, she is a natural born leader with an essentially combative style. She has met ignorance, ridicule and prejudice and battled back with irreverence, resilience and courage.

Baroness Trumpington

*'You don't think I am going to call myself Lady Six-Mile Bottom do
you?' (To Garter King of Arms)*

*****

Didn't she appear as the redoubtable aunt of 'Catsmeat' Potter-
Pirbright in *Right Ho! Jeeves*? Or was Lady Trumpington the sister of
Bertie Wooster's Aunt Dahlia in *Galahad at Blandings*? The name has
an unmistakable P G Wodehousian familiarity to it.

But this is a case of nature imitating art. Jean Barker, the Baroness
Trumpington of Sandwich, is for real. The vision exactly mirrors the
sonority and solidity of the name. Tall and imposing, with large feet
planted firmly facing outwards, her voice booms and reverberates
around the Gothic halls and corridors of the House of Lords.

When Jean was made a peer she discussed with Garter King of
Arms (the senior herald of the College of Arms), suitable place-
names with a Cambridge connection for use in her title – in
particular Trumpington, the village she had once represented on
the City Council. A Barony of Trumpington had apparently once
been granted to someone else (although the line had died out
centuries before). 'Is there another place near Cambridge you
would like?' the herald enquired hopefully. 'What about the village
where you now live?' She exploded with mirth, 'You don't think I
am going to call myself Lady Six Mile Bottom, do you?' With that,
Garter duly surrendered and Lady Trumpington she became.

She might be a relic of an earlier age – the kind of product of

Empire and Raj who ought to be seen riding aloft in an elephant howdah, descending by trunk to dispense thunderingly good sense to the natives. A matter-of-fact heroine born to repel dervishes or resist the siege of some remote British legation with phlegmatic courage and a pot of tea.

She was born in 1922. Her father was a Bengal Lancer who became ADC to a Viceroy of India; her mother, a large extrovert American, born in England. Her mother was well off until the slump, when she lost everything. 'We lived a rather odd life, just one round of extravagance, until suddenly we had no money at all.' Her mother's idea of economy was to 'take a bus to the Ritz'.

All little girls want to be ballet dancers, naturally envying the lithe movements and supple grace of a ballerina. Jean was no exception but, alas, she was no sugar-plum fairy and the pink ballet shoes were discarded in favour of green gum boots. Her second preference was to be a vet. Her father decreed she should start by studying frogs – so she was packed off to examine the art and literature of France.

During the war she was sent to gain experience on Lloyd George's farm at Churt in Surrey. Some girls had rather more intimate experiences of the legendary 'old goat' than others. Jean did her duty as a Land Girl, emerged with virtue intact, and left to join the code-breaking teams at Bletchley Park, specialising in the analysis of German naval signals. Her bluff and jovial exterior belies a sharp brain and she is a formidably good bridge player.

After the war she was secretary to Viscount Hinchingbrooke MP for a couple of years and then set off to America with £5 in her pocket. Her ingenious way of surviving until the first pay cheque arrived was to gorge on cocktail snacks at receptions and parties so that she never needed to buy proper food. 'I never met anyone at all for the first few weeks . . . I was so busy eating as much as I could.'

She did stop eating long enough to meet one person who was to form the backbone of her life, Alan Barker, a Cambridge don who was a visiting Fellow at Yale. Love blossomed amongst the canapés and cocktail-sticks. They married back in England, soon moving to Eton where Alan became a master, and then to Cambridge upon his appointment as headmaster of the Leys School.

Mrs Barker took to school life like a gin to tonic and she provided the fizz. 'I loved it. No weekends off and our home was always public. The door was never shut. One did anything that was asked of one. One really was a mother figure.' 'I loved the boys and, having been rather naughty at school myself, always had sympathy with the baddies – and so many of the baddies have turned out great successes in life.' What spiffing good luck for those boys, who found themselves under the care of such a magnificent surrogate mother.

Both her parents were active Liberals and she was brought up in a political atmosphere. She tried to get into Parliament as a Conservative but encountered an 'East Anglian hostility to women MPs'. So she immersed herself in local politics as a substitute, rising to become a redoubtable Mayor of Cambridge.

Shortly after retiring as Mayor, Jean paid a visit to the National Stud at nearby Newmarket. As she approached the box of a stallion called Hopeful Venture, the horse sensed her pleasurable presence and began to exhibit the normal red-blooded male equine's signs of arousal. Suddenly, it wasn't just the media who were interested in covering Mrs Barker. The Director of the National Stud, Colonel Douglas Gray, asked with some embarrassment whether she was wearing scent because, if stallions evince no amorous interest, an aphrodisiac scent is put on the mares. 'Not only am I wearing scent,' she declared, 'but I am also an Ex-Mayor.'

Her delight at being elevated to the Lords in 1981 was palpable and endearing. 'I feel terribly grateful to be there.' She was introduced by veteran Tory peers, Peter Thorneycroft and Rab Butler, and took the oath in her throatily resonant Capstan Full-Strength voice.

From the outset she made a name for herself as a 'card', a charmingly unconventional member of the Establishment. 'I like to make life as enjoyable as possible and the element of fun gives one, in a curious way, more influence. People listen to you because they are not sure what's coming next.'

Their Lordships certainly loved her lively contributions to their debates, never quite knowing what she might say next. In a discussion on the Elgin Marbles Lord Glenamara proposed that they should be handed back to Greece. He received a tart and succinct retort, 'My Lords, I do not agree with the Noble Lord. In fact, his remarks rather bring into doubt his own marbles.'

She enraged the animal welfare lobby by suggesting that unmapped minefields, left by the Argentines in the Falklands, should be cleared by driving flocks of sheep across the barren acres as sacrificial mine detectors. The predictably outraged letter from the RSPCA was countered with a common-sense reply, 'My point was that sheep could quickly be put out of their misery and eaten whereas men could not.'

Her remarks did much to improve the profitability of the Post Office, by provoking a torrent of letters. One correspondent wrote calling her a 'fat old scrubber', a description which caused the Noble Baroness great mirth and which she gloried in repeating. Innovative as the idea was, it proved not to be a winner. The Ministry of Defence dismissed it with the explanation that 'sheep are not heavy enough'.

When steaming full ahead she is as difficult to turn about as a fully laden oil tanker. After speaking from the Dispatch Box in the Lords as the relevant Minister on a complicated amendment to be made in a Social Security Bill, she suddenly announced, 'Oh dear! I've just been talking utter balls!' She added that she had been speaking inadvertently from notes on a quite different amendment and that her speech had had nothing whatever to do with the matter under discussion. Either their Lordships had been too polite to intervene to draw this to her attention or, in the soporific slumbering atmosphere, no one had noticed. If she had not thought to mention it, the whole incident would probably have subsided unnoticed into the annals of *Hansard* and, had there been a division, she could well have enjoyed a massive majority in support of a wholly erroneous proposition.

In an inspired appointment, she was later made an Agriculture Minister – rather like a Joyce Grenfell sketch made flesh in well-upholstered tweeds and green wellies. She was straight out of Central Casting for the role of striding across acres of grouse moor, prodding a Gloucester Old Spot or discussing the price of mangelwurzels. In this job she was also Minister of Food. She exulted, 'I love all those high-cholesterol breakfast dishes' – but sadly had to confess 'I don't eat breakfast any more.' But, even if forbidden to indulge, she could luxuriate in the thought. While reading the lesson at King's College, Cambridge Carol Service she subconsciously strayed from her text into saying 'A little lamb shall feed them', instead of 'A little lamb shall lead them.' 'Trust you Mum,' said her son, 'to think of food.'

It comes as no surprise to learn from Lady Trumpington: 'I like my beef bloody and my lamb pink . . . I think food should be well presented but I can do without it looking like a Gauguin. Summer pudding is the greatest pudding ever invented. I love good sausages and there's an awful lot you can do with mince.' She is perfectly at home in the House of Lords, where tastes tend to have reached a peak of sophistication in adolescence if not the nursery, and the favourite dishes are reputed to be steak and kidney pudding and spotted dick.

In 1989 the noble Baroness gave a bravura demonstration of her pioneer spirit when she became the first British Minister to make an official visit to Ulan Bator, capital of Outer Mongolia. As Minister of Food she was intrigued for a few days to enjoy the local diet of dried mutton and rancid yak's milk, relieved only by the occasional vegetable which Her Britannic Majesty's Ambassador had managed to coax out of the sparse soil of his Embassy allotment.

She also visited a school, genially inviting the children to try out their English by asking her questions. There was particular interest in two: 'How old are you?' and 'What is your telephone number?' Now that privatisation has reached even to Outer Mongolia, perhaps the local equivalent of BT has managed to wire up every 'yurt' (the traditional circular tent of skins stretched across poles, in which the nomadic population still lives).

Social life on the steppe must have been transformed by modern communications, making it possible to ring up your neighbouring herdsman to say, 'Fancy a glass of yak's milk in my yurt?' Despite this spur to Mongolian merriment, whereas 'Bring a bottle' parties used to be all the rage in London, 'bring a yak' parties have never caught on in quite the same way in downtown Ulan Bator.

Jean did her bit brilliantly for international diplomacy. British-Mongolian relations never looked back. President Punsalmaagiin Orchirbat of Mongolia paid a return visit personally shortly afterwards, calling on the Queen and visiting Leeds, Britain's equivalent of Ulan Bator (equivalent only in being its twin town, I hasten to add, before sales of this book plummet in Yorkshire!).

For a time she also answered in the Lords for the Department of National Heritage and, as such, was surrogate Minister of Sport. She is not aerodynamically constructed for certain types of sport e.g. slalom racing and gymnastic displays on the parallel bars. But she is ideal for others where deft movement is not quite so central to success. She was a keen supporter of the annual Lords and Commons Charity Tug-o'-War.

As the Cheer Leader for the House of Lords team, she inspired them to victory, flailing her pink pom-poms in the air like the propeller of a Spitfire. Her deep-throated roar could be heard across Westminster urging the puffing and perspiring peers successfully onwards to victory.

She once sent a warm letter of condolence to a fellow peer, following the death of his wife. Seeing her in the corridors a few days later he naturally thanked her for her concern. However, he also explained that as his wife was alive and well the letter was, perhaps, a little superfluous. 'Never mind,' said Jean. 'Keep the letter. It will come in useful one day.'

As an admirer of well-developed masculinity, her knowledge usually applied in appreciation of the fetlocks of a stallion, she was once at a rock-music award ceremony in London when a young man with bare, tanned, muscular legs walked past. Pointing with uninhibited enthusiasm, she was clearly heard to say, 'Cor! Just look at those!' It may be a surprise that she was often found at such events, eagerly asking, 'Is Elton John here?' or whether the latest badly behaved teeny-bopper group sensation has arrived. She had not become a superannuated groupie but she is an inveterate autograph hunter – on behalf of her secretary – and has no qualms about buttonholing such important figures.

She is not overawed by anyone or anything. But neither is she overawing. No one could be more tolerant or sympathetic. Her self-deprecation makes friends even amongst the most extreme of her political adversaries. She exudes informality, as when she made her maiden appearance as Heritage spokesman in the Lords dealing with a Question on broadcasting. Being completely unfamiliar with her new brief, she openly expressed concern that 'I might get my knickers in a twist.' Unrecorded by *Hansard*, apparently their Lordships broke into a chant of 'Marks & Spencer, Marks & Spencer' – clearly, under all that ermine, they are the same as 95 per cent of the population.

During the debate on the Maastricht Treaty she quelled a mini-riot on the back benches as their Noble Lordships fought to be heard. 'My Lords behave yourselves. One at a time. We will have the Lord Campbell, then we will have the Lord Beloff.' Her tone brooked no argument and they duly fell into line, like unruly schoolboys sorted out by matron.

Never lost for words, she filled in as warm-up artiste for a colleague in the following way: 'My Lords, I stand before you metaphorically naked because I am awaiting the Noble Lord, Lord Lucas. I can think of various ways in which I can regale your Lordships, but I am happy to see my Noble Friend and so can sit down.'

Hers is a formidable presence and she is tirelessly devoted to good and worthy causes. She was an early advocate of the pooper-scooper for dogs and also of Sunday trading. 'What sense is there in a law which says a mother may buy a bottle of gin on a Sunday but not milk for her baby's bottle; a newspaper from a newsagent but not a Bible from a bookshop.'

Tragically, her husband was paralysed by a stroke in the mid-1980s and he was, to her dismay, unable to participate in much of Jean's new life in the Lords. She observed sadly, 'My status has changed, I am neither a wife, nor a widow nor a single person. I find that I have had to become much more independent than I used to be.' This has caused its fair share of problems but she is irrepressibly practical.

She recounts one example: 'Living with a disabled person means you have to think ahead about all kinds of little things. For example I was coming home in a taxi the other night and I thought I would probably have some trouble with the zip of my dress. So I asked the taxi driver if he could unzip it for me. He thought I was mad at first, but I explained the situation and he agreed on condition that I didn't scream!' He need not have worried – anyone accused of sexually harassing Lady Trumpington is much more likely to be awarded the VC than a prison sentence.

Although most women are sensitive about their figure and they know all about being different sizes at different times, only Jean Trumpington could label her own wardrobes as 'Outsize' 'Fat' and 'Obese'!

Like many of the Battleaxes, Lady Trumpington admits to being less tough than many might think. 'Self confident? It's a bit on the surface you know. I am more sensitive than would appear.'

She is always the first to laugh at herself but warns against people not taking her seriously. 'I don't like it when I'm portrayed as just a big giggle.' If provoked one might just find that the Barker is worse than the bite. I wouldn't recommend trying it on just to find out.

Eve Pollard

'You just have to believe you're right. I'm terribly impatient. I want everything yesterday.'
*****

Clement Freud described Eve Pollard as 'a substantial woman. "Avoirdupois" is the word that sprang to mind. Nothing so common as "big".'

'Battle Boobs', 'La Stupenda', 'Lady Bollard', 'Killer Bimbo of Fleet Street.' She is lampooned as over-bosomed, under-dressed, over-paid and over-powering. But, striding around her office in tight skirts, four-inch stilletos, and distractingly low-cut tops, Eve puts on a bold front and thrusts aside patronising sexist comment from the Old Adams of Fleet Street.

Eve and I have one common distinction. We have both been the butt of surprisingly sexist abuse from balding 'left-wing progressive' *Observer* hack, John Sweeney. It was he who said of me that 'to describe her as Lady Macbeth is to insult Lady Macbeth'.

Of La Bollard, he was even more insultingly direct: 'Take two of the large, white early-warning globes that adorn the North Yorkshire moors at Fylingdales. Hold the image in your mind. Now shoehorn them into a vacuum-packed glitzy dress, imperfectly buttoned-up. The reader may now begin to comprehend something of the enormity of Eve Pollard's breasts.' Eve is all too familiar with that male chauvinist stereotype: 'When men hear that I've got a new job they don't think "good business brain" they think "38 D-cup"'.

Eve Pollard

ATLAS

She is self-deprecating about her magnificent mammaries and admits her 'hopeless addiction to (her) cleavage'. However, her necklines have risen with her job, as she has scaled more up-market echelons of the newspaper world. Should she ever edit the *Financial Times*, Fleet Street's first front would probably disappear under a polo-neck – a most unjournalistic transition from exposure to cover-up.

Eve Pollard (more properly Lady Lloyd – she is married to Sir Nicholas Lloyd) concedes she is probably a demanding and difficult boss. She enjoys her reputation for eating men at breakfast and spitting them out for lunch. She rides all jokes about being 'Lady Muck'. Being Lady Lloyd hardly impinges. 'I don't think anyone I know addresses me as Lady. When I hear it, I don't quite believe it. But, always having used my maiden name, I never quite used to believe I was Mrs Lloyd either.'

Her philosophy is simple: 'Every now and then you find someone who just doesn't agree with you. They may not be wrong but you just have to believe you're right.' 'I'm terribly impatient. I want everything yesterday.'

She was a bookworm as a child, fascinated by the written word. Her mother was Viennese; her Hungarian father an inventor who disapproved of women going to University. They worked together actively running a company. Her mother provided Eve with a powerful role-model to go out and succeed herself. She left school at 18, entered a publishing house and never looked back.

She rose through the publishing world like a 1960s hemline. Starting as Assistant to the Fashion Editor of *Honey* in 1967, she moved on to *Petticoat* and into newspapers at the *Daily Mirror*. By 1970 she was Women's Editor of the *Observer* colour supplement and, from 1971–81, Women's Editor of the *Sunday Mirror*. She was a campaigning Editor, and, in her spare time, wrote a best-seller about Jackie Kennedy.

During the 1980s she surged around the world of Fleet Street, television and magazines. The *Sunday People*, *TV-AM*, launching *Elle* in the States, *News of the World* colour supplement, *Mail on Sunday* magazine – and then, in 1988, she arrived as Editor of the *Sunday Mirror*, handpicked by 'Cap'n Bob' Maxwell himself.

History does not relate whether he tried to get his hands on her assets. If he did, she was more than a match for him, using every ounce of feminine guile at her disposal but unafraid to shout back and win.

In 1991 she slipped effortlessly from the socialist *Mirror* to Tory *Sunday Express*, becoming the first woman to edit a mid-market national newspaper. Her husband was at that time Editor of the *Daily Express*, creating a unique double act. The *Express* was ailing, with a rapidly declining circulation of 1.6 million. Many of the readers were dying off week by week without new, younger ones being attracted in their place.

The paper confirmed the prejudices of middle-aged, middle-England but did not attract their offspring. For many, the profile of the new Editor was higher and better known than that of the newspaper. She said 'There's nothing wrong with older readers; they have a lot of money and a lot of free time for leisure. I don't want to alienate them. I just want to replace the ones who are dying.'

She is aggressively feminine and arrived for her first day reportedly dressed as an admiral, resplendent in short, tight navy skirt and ocean-going jacket with brocade, frogging, epaulettes. The only thing she lacked was the telescope.

With 'a penchant for promotional hype that would make a huckster blush' she set about her task of increasing circulation. With the backing of journalists and many commentators, she fought chairman, Lord Stevens of Ludgate, to force through the controversial decision to shrink the paper from a broadsheet to a tabloid. It seemed to work and, just a year after her appointment, the paper was named Newspaper of the Year. In 1993 it was Sunday Newspaper of The Year.

Eve was delighted to learn that, following her appointment to the *Express*, Lord Rothermere gave the arch-rival *Mail on Sunday* an additional £5m to counter whatever she might throw at them. 'I saw Lord Rothermere and said "Is it true about the £5 million?" and he said "Oh, much more than that", which is just so sweet.'

Lord Stevens was not prepared to commit the necessary money to take on the *Mail*, which was outspending the *Express* in almost every department and pouring millions into TV and other promotions. Without the money to pay for top-flight writers, to retain the best production staff, to bid for exciting serialisations etc. Eve was fighting with at least one hand tied behind her back.

Lord Stevens created a difficulty for Eve because, unlike so many of her readers, he was not dying off. A hard-nosed businessman with no ink in his veins, on one occasion he apparently reduced Eve to tears in a furious argument. Unmoved by the pathos of the display, he coldly observed, 'Now you know how your staff feel.'

In spite of the easy-going charm and femininity, she is a tough, sharp businesswoman as well as journalist. Early on in her career at the *Sunday Express*, a putative interviewer was told by one of Eve's staff 'She's too busy sacking people to give interviews.' She had to wait a year and a half before an audience was granted and, on arrival, was ushered onto a low sofa while La Bollard dominated the scene, towering over her from a high chair behind the desk.

The story that she sent out a senior male member of staff to buy her red nail varnish has not been authenticated. However, under Eve the *Express* was no Garden of Eden. Staff turnover was high and morale low – largely because the paper's sales, after an initial fillip, remained in decline. Disaffection amongst staff led to a constant flow of damaging stories in *Private Eye*, which hummed with the sound of axes being ground. One grumbler said, 'It's been like working in a prison camp.' An impromptu but wild party was thrown at a local hostelry to celebrate her departure from the *Express* in 1994.

This coincided with another dispute with Lord Stevens. One theory held that she annoyed Lady Stevens by insisting on publishing an 'unhelpful' story about the Princess of Wales, a chum of Her Ladyship. Stevens allegedly vetoed a scoop story for the *Daily Express* about Diana making anonymous nuisance phone calls to a friend of her husband. When it became clear, three days later, that the *News of the World* was going to splash the story, reluctantly he allowed the *Sunday Express* to carry it. Eve is supposed to have annoyed Lord and Lady Stevens by the headline 'Diana Phone Pest Riddle', which was held to imply acceptance that Diana had indeed made the disputed calls.

Diana denied the story in an interview in the *Daily Mail* the following day. She offered a string of alibis for the dates and times when the calls were supposed to have been made. On one of these occasions she revealed that she had been 'lunching in Mayfair with Lady Stevens, wife of newspaper proprietor, Lord Stevens'.

Whether this disagreement lit the blue touch paper or not, it was the culmination of three years of altercation. One staff member said, 'There's been a thrill, a spill or a crisis every week. It's very unsettling for a newspaper in decline as ours is.'

Eve Pollard may have been out but she is far from down. As she says 'They can always have a go at you on account of the way you look. I always joked that I knew I'd hit the wrong side of *Private Eye* when they stopped calling me La Stupenda and called me Lady Bollard. What we have to do is learn not to care.'

Eve is multi-talented. Having retired, only temporarily I am sure, from the full limelight, she is joint-author of two bestselling novels, the aptly titled *Splash* and *Best of Enemies*, and is now the Agony Aunt for the *Mirror*, dispensing common sense advice to those sensible enough to ask for it.

Queen Boadicea
(d.circa AD 61)

'I am fighting . . . for my lost freedom, my bruised body and my outraged daughters . . . the gods will grant us the vengeance we deserve.'

*****

Boadicea (Boudicca to orthographical pedants) was Queen of the Iceni, a tribe of Britons living in East Anglia, in the years following the Roman colonisation of Britain. Boadicea's husband, King Prasutagus, had become a Roman client-king. He attempted to appease the Roman conquerors and to preserve his kingdom from attack after his death by bequeathing half his wealth to Emperor Nero, leaving a quarter each to his two daughters.

Boadicea appears not to have been a beneficiary under his will at all. But before she could get down to the local CAB for advice on how to register a claim under the Inheritance (Provision for Family and Dependants) Act, the Romans decided to absorb Prasutagus' kingdom into their province. They then systematically 'plundered like prizes of war' both the kingdom and royal household.

In AD 60 she raised the standard of revolt against Roman oppression. She was an impressive figure. Cassius Dio, a Roman historian writing about AD 200, described her formidable mane of bright red hair, harsh voice, terrifying aspect, huge frame and 'notoriety of having put men to shame . . . she grasped a spear to strike fear into all who watched her.' After cataloguing Rome's bloodsoaked humiliations at the hands of the first known British Battleaxe he whimpered with rueful political incorrectness: 'All this ruin was brought upon the Romans by a WOMAN.'

Boadicea was flogged, her daughters raped, the Iceni chiefs were deprived of their hereditary estates and the king's relatives were reduced to slavery – all of which did not make for harmonious community relations with the local inhabitants. Further humiliations heaped upon the whole tribe were so intolerable that they provoked a rebellion rather than merely a complaint to the Quaestio Perpetua Aequalitatis Gentilis (Commission for Racial Equality).

Boadicea decided to besiege and sack Camelodunum (Colchester), the largest Roman settlement in the area. The town had been created by Roman military veterans who simply expelled the previous Iceni inhabitants, seized their lands and built on them – provoking predictable festering resentment. Other aggrieved tribes, like the Trinovantes, then joined the rebellion.

The Britons had been encouraged by various omens. The Roman statue of victory at Camelodunum fell down 'with its back turned as if it were fleeing the enemy'. Delirious women chanted of destruction at hand. They cried that in the local senate house outlandish yells had been heard; the theatre had echoed with shrieks; at the mouth of the Thames a phantom settlement had been seen in ruins. A blood-red colour in the sea and shapes like human corpses left by the ebb tide were interpreted as signs of hope by the Britons and signs of disaster by the Roman defenders.

Boadicea routed a Roman division and forced the imperial procurator, Catus Decianus, to flee to Gaul. London and St Albans, left undefended, were sacked and burnt like Colchester. According to Tacitus more than 70,000 were killed in the three towns 'for the barbarians would have no capturing, no selling, nor any kind of traffic usual in war; they would have nothing but killing, by sword, cross, gibbet or fire.' Sir Winston Churchill observed approvingly of Boadicea's policy: 'it is the primary right of men to die and kill for the land they live in, and to punish with exceptional severity all members of their own race who have warmed their hands at the invaders' hearth.'

In due course Suetonius Paulinus, the Roman Governor of
Britain, who had been busy massacring the druids of Anglesey,
assembled an army of 10,000 Roman regular soldiers plus
auxiliaries and marched south to put down the rebellion. He chose
his ground, probably near Lichfield, so that he could be attacked
only from the front. The Britons were so confident of victory that
they assembled their women and children in wagons at the edge of
the battlefield to observe the spectacle, as though it was the Royal
Tournament at Earls Court.

Tacitus describes in his *Annals of Imperial Rome* how Boadicea
inspired her troops:

'Boadicea drove round all the tribes in a chariot with her
daughters in front of her. "We British are used to women
commanders in war," she cried. "I am descended from mighty men!
But I am not fighting for my kingdom and wealth now. I am
fighting as an ordinary person for my lost freedom, my bruised
body and my outraged daughters. But the gods will grant us the
vengeance we deserve! The Roman division which dared to fight is
annihilated. The others cower in their camps or watch for a chance
to escape . . . Consider how many of you are fighting – and why!
Then you will win this battle,or perish. That is what I, a woman,
plan to do! – let the men live in slavery if they will."'

Suetonius' superior tactics put Boadicea's troops to flight but
their retreat was inhibited by the wagons of women and children
out for the day. All were slaughtered. Boadicea escaped but, to
avoid capture and humiliation, committed suicide, probably by
taking poison.

The British Warrior Queen's heroism survived in folk memory
and was commemorated in literature, notably in the lines of the
eighteenth-century poet, William Cowper:

> *'Regions Caesar never knew*
> *Thy posterity shall sway,*
> *Where his eagles never flew*
> *None invincible as they.*
>
> *Such the bard's prophetic words*

> *Pregnant with celestial fire*
> *Bending, as he swept the chords*
> *Of his sweet but awful lyre.*
>
> *She, with all a monarch's pride,*
> *Felt them in her bosom glow;*
> *Rushed to battle, fought and died;*
> *Dying, hurled them at the foe.*
> *"Ruffians, pitiless as proud,*
> *Heaven awards the vengeance due;*
> *Empire is on us bestowed,*
> *Shame and ruin wait for you."'*

Boadicea's grave was recently located by archaeologists – who believe that it is under platform eight at King's Cross railway station. On 22 February 1988 the *Daily Telegraph* reported the reaction of British Rail to this news: 'We have just refurbished platform eight and anyone wanting to dig it up had better come up with a strong case.'

Gertrude Shilling

'The Mascot of Ascot. The Dowager of Fashion and Grande Dame of Ladie's Day.'

*****

Lewis Carroll's Mad Hatter sported a price ticket of ten shillings and sixpence in his topper. Mad hats have been associated with two Shillings at Royal Ascot every year since 1961. Mrs Gertrude Shilling has been delighting the crowds by wearing the newest monstrous creations of her son David. If he were in the Government he would be the Prime Milliner.

In equal measure they have delighted the populace and enraged the stuffed shirts of the Jockey Club and the Royal Enclosure. 'I am not in favour of these exotic performances,' sniffed Lord Willoughby de Broke, aged 83.

Dubbed by her son as The Mascot of Ascot, she is the Dowager of Fashion and Grande Dame of Ladies' Day. 'I only come to see the Queen,' she confides. 'As soon as I've done that I'm off home. I haven't seen a race for years – not since my husband Ronald died in 1984.'

David is the world-famous Hatter and her desire to advertise his wares is matched only by a desire to advertise herself. She succeeds spectacularly in both departments. Royalty and the rich lose their heads for his hats all over the world. They can command thousands of pounds apiece.

But his most outrageous creations are reserved for his faithful mother. Indeed who else would or could wear them with such aplomb? For his sake (and just possibly to draw attention to herself) she has been prepared to wear virtually anything, even a four-foot high giraffe's head, and it is David, rather than she, who occasionally puts his foot down at her more outlandish suggestions.

She began quietly enough. Even as late as in 1969 she made a relatively modest appearance on the first day with a four-foot topper. By 1971 she had decided to turn her hand to modelling. She rang the Ugly Agency who demanded 'Are you ugly?' 'I am hideous', came the reply. 'Will you take me on your books?' They did and her first job paid eight guineas for an hour's modelling of a pink hat and outfit to advertise Babycham. Sparing the nation, she declined to do 'nudies' but would stick only to fully clothed work.

In 1972 she announced that Ascot was 'old hat'. She retired from the racecourse and moved into the theatre. She signed on for drama classes, hoping to find a niche in Old Time Music Hall. She did appear here and there, notably at the Theatre Royal in Stratford East. But the lure of Ascot proved too much and, to the mixed delight and horror of racegoers, she came back with a vengeance.

In 1973 Europe went to her head. She lifted the thoughts of the crowd from the grey skies and drizzle of the opening day with a celebration of Britain joining the EEC. The hat was a wondrous white creation, five feet in diameter and covered with the names in large black letters of all the nine member countries of the Common Market. It was so vast it had to be conveyed to Ascot in a van.

With her encouragement, it is small wonder Edward Heath took us into Europe. If only Gertrude had been on the side of the anti-marketeers she might have given them a head start and how different things might have been. That hat may have turned the tide of history.

1974 saw her again at her bizarre best with a room-sized hat in bilious orange, drooping under the weight of an endless feather boa of similar hue. The dress underneath defied the descriptive powers of most of the fashion writers, but appeared to have been an orange and gold pattern satin number in the style of a ship's figurehead.

In 1977 she went indisputably too far and was denied entry to the Royal Enclosure. Her patriotic red, white and blue hat, to celebrate the Queen's Silver Jubilee, was four feet high and seven feet across. The gatekeeper, Mr Sam Gillespie, defended himself by saying his decision had nothing to do with taste. The hat simply would not get through the gate. He did, however, permit himself an aesthetic judgment and declared it 'a monstrosity'.

Away from the racetrack, in October 1977 she lent her considerable weight to the late Sir Keith Joseph's campaign to cut out over-manning in public departments. She wrote to *The Times* (then a paper of record) bewailing the fact that a recalcitrant mouse in her husband's factory had hitherto been dealt with swiftly and effectively by poison and the Hackney Health Department, whereas the current nuisance was still running amok while the same Health Department was sending forms, forms and more forms but no poison. If only her hat collection had included a bowler with a lead-lined brim, like Odd Job in Ian Fleming's *Dr No!* she could have dealt the recalcitrant rodent a fatal blow with a battlehat.

In 1980 the family shirt business collapsed because it could not compete with cheap imports. But that tragedy did nothing to diminish Mrs Shilling's enthusiasm for life in general and Ascot in particular. She made it abundantly clear that, although she had lost her shirt, she still had her hats and her lifestyle would continue come what may. It was warm for Ascot and her relatively modest but outsize pink feather hat rippled happily in the welcome breeze.

In 1982 even her son, David, drew the line at one of her ideas; a headpiece to celebrate the forthcoming royal birth. Something pink and blue, to cover all eventualities, with a stork and a baby dangling around. Thank heavens for wiser counsel. She was diverted into a more tastefully patriotic direction.

The Falklands War had been won and, in the good old days, everyone would have been dressed appropriately to welcome 'our victorious boys' back home. Mrs Shilling did not disappoint. Within hours of the ceasefire her son created a scarlet hooped-skirt with a red white and blue Victory hat, sporting a dove of peace and two Union Flags which looked hideously dangerous in a gusty wind. Nigel Dempster tastelessly suggested it might have been better to depict the sinking of the *Belgrano*.

She vehemently denies being turned away from the Royal

Enclosure in 1984 because the Stewards were not prepared to tolerate the outrageous confection. The hat was quite an eyecatcher. It did not require early warning radar to detect her approach. A dazzling four-foot wide dartboard (complete with darts), was set at an alarmingly rakish angle on her head. As she approached the gate the Clerk of the Course, Captain the Hon Nicholas Beaumont, was seen in urgent consultation with a bowler-hatted figure who was dispatched at a trot to bar her way. He is reported to have told her, with the utmost restraint and politeness, 'I am afraid you cannot come in here Madam, wearing that hat.'

One year Dame Edna Everage was tempted to compete. Down Under's most celebrated artiste wore Up Top an equally monstrous creation resembling the Sydney Opera House. The Dame sidled up to Mrs Shilling and told her she had lipstick smeared all over her teeth. 'Forgive me for saying so but these things are important to us girls.'

One of her offerings in 1984 was in honour of the Olympic Games; combining five coloured rings and a red perspex symbolic flame, it was even more ludicrous than normal. It caught the eye of the Queen Mother who prodded Princess Margaret and, in a chain reaction, the eyes of the entire Royal procession turned to stare. Mrs Shilling was delighted and could go home before the first race.

1992 saw an ingenious four-foot sunflower with battery-powered canary. In 1994 she was dressed to kill in her mermaid outfit: a long tubular turquoise blue sequinned dress with the usual arrestingly titanic hat around which frolicked starfish, seahorses and all manner of underwater flora and fauna. You could positively smell the sea as she wafted past.

The previous day she had worn another long sequinned number in silver with medals dotted all over it. She called it her D-Day outfit, but one commentator unkindly described her as more closely resembling a mackerel trussed up in tin foil for baking.

In 1996, she emerged on the Friday under what was a seriously extraordinary creation, even for her. A length of gold piping was coiled turban-like around her head and rose above it like a cobra's head poised to strike. It was a shower, complete with large nozzle spraying a veil of 'water' (described by one fashion writer as 'cobwebs') over her face. One day earlier in the week she had arrived barely visible under a towering spiral of black and white Brighton Rock.

She is, of course, ludicrous. But she can laugh at herself and tells an amusing tale from her distant past. As a young woman she was strolling in the Royal Hospital Gardens when a handsome man came up to her, grasped her in passionate embrace, smothered her in kisses, and whispered, 'Darling, thank goodness you were able to come.'

She managed to release his grasp and pointed out that if he took a closer look he would realise he had made a mistake. Thirty-five years later she met the same man at a Foyles Literary Luncheon. Asked if he remembered the incident, his eyes sparkled with laughter: 'How amusing! But sadly I cannot remember,' said Sir John Gielgud.

It is in fighting illness that Gertrude has shown true grit and determination. Her bravery is an example to women everywhere. After all, anyone can wear a silly hat to Ascot and thousands do every year. In the 1960s Gertrude battled against the disease which strikes terror into the hearts of most women, breast cancer, and has fought it off twice since then. She has battled against crippling illness and, now in her eighties, was near death at the turn of this year. Her heart stopped beating but she came through and was able to be at Ascot as normal, wearing a creation called 'Bird's Nest Soup' complete with silver eggs and birds with Union Flag wings. David puts her determination down to 'the fear of not living life to the full – as strong as her fear of death.'

Battle on Mrs Shilling. Hats off to you and delight us all at Ascot next year.

Violet Carson

Miss Violet Carson OBE
aka Ena Sharples
(b.1898 – d.1983)

'My name is Ena Sharples. I'm caretaker of the Glad Tidings Mission 'all. And, by the way, you owe me an egg.'

*****

Coronation Street – the programme which, since 1960, has showed the upper and middle classes how nicely the working classes are doing, thank you – revolved for twenty years around the unreconstructed dragon, Ena Sharples, who convincingly personified the southern myth of the aggressive, rude northerner.

Described by Bill Roache (Ken Barlow) as 'an actress who combined great natural dignity and strength of character with a face you could break rocks on', she was the very embodiment of *Coronation Street*. Ruling the roost from her corner in the Snug Bar at the Rovers Return, glass of milk stout gripped firmly as a truncheon in her hand, she scowled ferociously with crag visage at all and sundry. With a hairnet appearing to be made of barbed-wire and a lip which seemed permanently curled in an expression of furious distaste, she was as cuddly as a scorpion.

Her constant companion, minuscule, mousy Minnie Caldwell, who frequently seemed on the verge of tears, was the perfect foil. Everyone was the butt of Ena's excoriating tongue and her dogged determination to poke her nose into other people's business. She was always ready to offer advice, usually unwanted, in a flagrantly aggressive way. Often she just offered flagrant aggression without the excuse of advice. She was the ultimate British Battleaxe and proud of it.

Violet Carson assumed the role of the pugnacious hairnetted harridan at the age of 61, after a lifetime of success in show business. She had been a silent film pianist (at the Ambassador Cinema in Pendleton), making a successful switch to 'wireless' in 1935 after the talkies had arrived. She achieved national fame as Auntie Vi on *Children's Hour* and secured a place in the nation's affections as 'Vi at the Piano' in Wilfred Pickles' radio series *Have a Go*. By 1950 she was one of the most versatile personalities on radio and claimed to have 'done almost everything on the BBC except read the news and the epilogue'.

Both her parents were musical and Violet's artistry at the piano moved her audience alternately to laughter or tears. In one programme alone (*Violet's Day Out*) she played a piano concerto with the BBC Northern Symphony Orchestra, sang a song from *Carmen*, accompanied herself in a classical aria, and rounded the whole thing off with some rollicking old-time music hall numbers.

She adapted to all technological developments, effortlessly switching to television when it began to overtake the radio in the 1950s. She was an established actress long before *Coronation Street* was a twinkle in the eye of its creator, Tony Warren.

When *Coronation Street* was conceived, the casting of Ena Sharples had proved a tough nut to crack. After 24 actresses had been rejected, there was serious danger of the character being dropped. Then Tony Warren suddenly remembered Violet Carson, 'the actress who had smacked my bottom when I was a 12 year old actor in a radio play'. The Ena problem was instantly solved.

Violet was unimpressed with the character of Ena, whom she thought was 'just a back street bitch'. She signed for a thirteen-week season but stayed for 20 years, recording over 2,000 performances. 'Ena' took over the rest of her life but, she claimed, had she known in advance, she would never have taken the part. When the *Street* was eighteen years old, Violet revealed her true feelings: 'I realise that *Coronation Street* has made me but, as an actress, I have been destroyed. That's the word to use and I use it quite fearlessly. Ena Sharples killed Violet Carson on Day One of *Coronation Street*. She has taken over. She rules my life. I've begged them to bury the old girl and let me go but they won't hear of it.'

Ena became a national institution almost overnight. She heralded her arrival with the words 'My name is Ena Sharples. I'm caretaker of the Glad Tidings Mission 'all. And, by the way, you owe me an egg.' Within a year she was an exhibit in Madame Tussauds (in Blackpool). The stage role had begun to consume the actress in public.

Violet protested that 'I leave her firmly in the dressing room when I go home'. But, when Ena collapsed at the end of one episode, she was showered with flowers, calls and cards from fans who failed to differentiate fantasy from reality. Again, when Ena was sacked as caretaker of the Glad Tidings Mission, she was inundated with job offers from all over Britain.

Twenty-five million people tuned in every Monday and Wednesday in Britain, although Violet herself never watched a single episode in which she appeared. The show was a success world-wide from Australia to Canada, and from Nigeria to Thailand. On a tour of Australia in 1968 a crowd of 150,000 (larger than for the Beatles) cheered when she arrived in Adelaide. In scenes reminiscent of a Roman Triumph the streets were blocked, rose petals strewn in her path and her car was followed by a queue of fans more than a mile long. Because of the throng she was forced to stop 50 yards short of her hotel and had to be carried in by police and tour organisers.

Violet, like Ena, sometimes looked life straight in the eye with an uncompromising glare. Never cowed by officialdom, in 1964 she battled with Dr Beeching, chairman of British Railways. No mean exponent of the axe himself, he savaged a large part of Britain's loss-making rail network in the 1960s. Violet travelled daily the 50 miles from home in Blackpool to the Granada Studios in Manchester. Part of Beeching's changes created new schedules which made her 5.45 p.m. homeward train frequently late. Whereas other passengers meekly signed a petition, Miss Carson had a blazing row with the station master and confronted the chairman himself, threatening to quit the *Street* if the timetables were not changed. For this one occasion she was pleased to play the stage part in real life and she railroaded Beeching into changing the timetable back again.

Known as the 'Queen of the North', she imperiously welcomed a reporter who came to interview her in the Granada canteen over a suitably large plateful of egg and chips: 'You've got a nerve coming here on our recording day. We've lynched people for less. Still, since you're here, you cheeky young monkey, you might as well make yourself useful and pass the vinegar.'

Violet was born in a stereotype of Coronation Street itself – a four-roomed tenement in Corporation Street, Manchester. The daughter of a Scottish miller, she married in Manchester Cathedral in 1926 but, two years later, was left a widow at the age of 30. She was a one-man girl and did not marry again. She had no sympathy with modern carnal obsessions: 'I think sex is an absolutely bloody bore. Everything seems to be equated with sex and I'm sick and tired of it. Why don't they leave it where it should be, up in the bedroom.'

Her screen *bête noire* was Elsie Tanner, against whom Ena battled to uphold the declining morals of the Street. Elsie had rather different views on sex. Ena was sharply outspoken about her behaviour: 'That Elsie Tanner, she were just the same during the War. Skirts up 'ere an' "got any gum, chum?"'

Ena's screen-family life was dismal, as her rasping, vicious tongue had alienated her two daughters, Vera and Madge. Her son died as a babe in arms and she had never remarried after her husband died in the Depression. Violet refused to allow Ena to remarry. She spent her days battling against authority – she organised a sit-in at the OAP hut to prevent its demolition and fought off improbable plans to open a night-club in the Street.

Lucrative as it was, Violet Carson resented the way Ena took over her life and, in the public perception, her persona. 'I have become Ena Sharples. But I don't want to be that old bag all my life. I want people to remember Violet Carson.' However, the hairnet prevailed and tour companies brought coach loads to ogle at the seaside cottage Violet shared with her sister.

She was allowed 'out' of *Coronation Street* to do a six month run of *Stars on Sunday*. Despite Granada's tough rules on such matters she won the day saying 'If I don't get some relief from playing the old girl I shall go daft in the head. I've only had two breaks from Ena in nine years.'

In 1978 she left Manchester's Midland Hotel ahead of the then Prime Minister, James Callaghan, of whose presence she was utterly oblivious. Seeing a waiting limousine ahead of her, door held open in readiness by a uniformed flunkey, she understandably assumed that it was for her. She climbed in and gave the chauffeur an address. Too terrified to disabuse her of the mistake, the chauffeur simply drove off as instructed – leaving the unfortunate Prime Minister to walk.

In real life she differed in many ways from her screen persona. She didn't drink stout or beer but preferred brandy and champagne. She wore sable coats rather than hairnets. Whereas Ena was belligerent and misanthropic, Violet Carson was warm and humorous, enjoying the company of friends and tending her rose garden. A floribunda rose in peach and biscuit with yellow reverse was named in her honour. Ena dressed with uncompromising plainness whereas Violet admitted to being just a little lavish on clothes, justifying this on the basis that she had 'rather an expensive figure'.

She became an OBE in 1965 and was granted the singular honour of switching on the Blackpool Illuminations. An Honorary Degree from Manchester University followed in 1973 for 'services to the region' – perhaps for so long misinforming the south about life in the north. Her fellow graduand, Simone de Beauvoir, (author of *The Second Sex* and mistress of Jean-Paul Sartre), made a somewhat unlikely partner.

In a surprisingly enterprising suggestion for a nationalised industry, the Gas Board at one stage proposed killing her off (Ena that is), suggesting that she should inadvertently be overcome by fumes from a gas fire. Fuming furiously herself, Violet thundered, 'I am here to stay. To kill me off would be plain daft. I'd like to blow up the person who had the crazy idea. Ena Sharples is indestructible.' The Gas Board, practical and phlegmatically unsentimental, coaxed that, 'Her death would have a massive impact on the public. Millions would then check for faults in their own appliances.'

In 1970 she collected a Supreme Actress Award just a week before she collapsed with pernicious anaemia. She put it down to overwork – 12 hours a day, including travelling from Blackpool to Manchester. However, continuing to avoid the murderous attentions of the Gas Board, she battled on for years. Her last appearance in the Street was in February 1980.

Although her role was kept open by regular references to her staying with an old friend in Lytham St Anne's, she was never able to return and slowly faded away. She died at her home in Blackpool on Boxing Day 1983, aged 85. In her will Violet left £1,000 to Manchester's Sharp Street Ragged School, where barefoot children used to be given a ticket for free clogs.

Christine Hamilton

'No one who crosses Christine Hamilton forgets it in a hurry. She is indeed a lioness who, if attacked, bares her claws and strikes out.'
*****

According to Ros Wynne Jones of the *Independent*, 'Visitors to the Cheshire home of Neil Hamilton are greeted by two uncompromising Tory women. The first, clearly visible through the glass panel on the front door, is Margaret Thatcher, a few inches short of life-size and seated on a low chair in the hall. The cardboard cut-out Baroness is for once in two dimensional contrast with the flesh and blood iron lady who answers the door. She is Christine Hamilton . . .

'. . . the Hyacinth Bucket of British politics', according to the *Sun*'s Jane Moore: 'Grown men – and, yes, even veteran war correspondents – visibly tremble under her forceful tones. She is afraid of nothing and no one in her fierce determination to protect her husband Neil. One rather suspects her husband wouldn't dare do anything she hadn't agreed to first. No one who crosses Christine Hamilton forgets it in a hurry. She is indeed a lioness who, if attacked, bares her claws and strikes out. But you can't help liking and admiring her for it.'

Less flatteringly, other hacks have called Christine 'Lady Macbeth', 'a bossy liability', 'Lady Muck', 'the Wife from Hell' and 'a tyrant'. These textual perverts have usually suffered the sharp edge of her tongue. From his vantage-point under her thumb, Neil

Christine Hamilton.

would say their epithets are about as accurate as weather-man Michael Fish's scoffing at forecasts of the catastrophic hurricane of 1987.

Reporters stalked her Cheshire home for weeks on end in the 1997 general election, provoking volcanic eruptions, like this one from the *Mirror*: 'Pointing at the crowd of reporters, she barked: "Get those greasy reptiles off the church daffodils", following that up with, "Why don't you get a proper job instead of shovelling sh**t?"' The hapless victim of this tirade actually turned out to be a perfectly decent chap and rather embarrassed about his unsavoury trade.

Neil became an MP in 1983 and a Government Minister in 1990. So in his early years in the House of Commons he was dominated by two bossy blondes – Margaret Thatcher and Christine. In 1994 he resigned from the Government in order to clear his name over 'cash for questions' allegations – a battle still being waged. He has now served a writ for libel on Mohamed Al Fayed personally and is determined to bring the matter to court.

When he sought re-election to Parliament in 1997 he and Christine became embroiled in one of the most extraordinary contests in modern electoral history. The Labour Party withdrew their own candidate in Tatton and persuaded the Liberals to follow suit. TV reporter Martin Bell, whose career had been sidelined by the BBC, was induced to stand in their place with their active support.

Bell was no independent as he claimed, and has now admitted that he received professional help from Labour spin-doctors throughout the campaign – indeed his early election literature was written by Tony Blair's press secretary Alistair Campbell. His daughter, Melissa, was actually spun off her feet by a spin-doctor and is now to be married to a Labour apparatchik who came up from Labour's communications HQ in London to work in dad's campaign.

For several weeks, as the Hamiltons attracted saturation media coverage, the general election seemed to be entirely about them. On 10 April 1997 Christine became a national and international celebrity. An otherwise deadly-dull election campaign was suddenly sparked into life by her televised eyeball-to-eyeball confrontation with the interloper, Martin Bell.

It was a brilliantly sunny spring day and Bell had called his first press conference – on Knutsford Heath (where Highwayman Higgins had hijacked stage-coaches in the last century). Inspired by history, Neil decided to hijack his press conference and confront him with a few pointed questions. Contrary to popular mythology, this was not Christine's idea and, in her own words, she just 'tagged along' with Neil. However, when they arrived, the sight of the sanctimonious Bell was just too much for her – and the first shots were fired in the Battle of Knutsford Heath.

One journalist summed up her performance: 'Those who witnessed Christine Hamilton's ambush of the hapless Martin Bell may have wondered how on earth we managed to lose the Empire. A visiting Martian, on the basis of his observation of the Tatton siege, would certainly have found it difficult to believe that women were once oppressed . . . the voice boomed out again and again: "Do you accept my husband is innocent?"' Another wrote: 'Mrs Hamilton may be seen as a weapon in the armoury of Tory Tatton. If a weapon then definitely high-explosive and deadly – exocet missile rather than pea-shooter.'

Although Neil lost his seat, in compensation he acquired a Battleaxe. In fact the media dubbed Christine 'Britain's best known Battleaxe'. The trouble with a reputation, however, is that you have to live up to it. So Christine wrote this book to find out what was expected of her.

Neil and Christine were married on the Lizard peninsula, at the farthest tip of Cornwall, on the Saturday before polling day in the 1983 general election campaign. Christine had been looking forward to a fortnight's honeymoon in Venice. Instead she had to make do with one night in the Exeter Crest Motor Lodge Hotel on the way back to five more days canvassing on the doorsteps of Cheshire. They had an election to fight. She had the unusual experience of sharing her honeymoon with 69,000 people. Neil consoled her by assuring her that life with him would be one long honeymoon!

Christine, like Neil, has derived great happiness from the strength of their marriage, which remains rock-solid despite all the ups and downs of political life, and particularly their recent traumas. Lurid novelists (and journalists) like to portray Westminster as the 'sex and sin palace by the Thames'. This is a compelling attraction for some, no doubt. The reality is rather different. The most impressive phallic symbol at Westminster is Big Ben. Christine is phlegmatic: 'I have seen the strains at Westminster but, if people took their marriage vows more seriously there wouldn't be so many problems. Our problems haven't brought Neil and me any closer because we couldn't be any closer. In the nicest possible way we take each other for granted.'

During emotionally testing times recently, Christine's much-publicised chutzpah earned the plaudit: 'Even by Tory wives' standards for "standing by" their man, Mrs Hamilton has played a blinder.' But she is not just emotionally resilient, she is physically fearless too.

She thinks nothing of jumping out of an aircraft – which she has done for charity. And, coming down to earth, she once took on and routed a gang of thugs who had viciously attacked an old University friend and former MP, Harvey Proctor. The Hamiltons are modest shareholders in his shirt business based in genteel Richmond, Surrey. They were just visiting the shop one day, when the violent miscreants swaggered in. Neil instinctively leapt into action to repel boarders, only to get his nose broken in the resulting fracas. Christine, undaunted, immediately chased the attackers out of the shop and down the street, raising a hue and cry as she went, eventually pinning them down as they tried to escape on a bus. They were prosecuted, convicted and sent to prison to reflect at leisure on the perils of being sliced up by a Battleaxe.

Neil first met Christine at a Conservative student conference when they were both 19 years old. It took place in the magnificent surroundings of Swinton Castle in Yorkshire. Christine looked quite at home among the battlements. Across a crowded room she spied Neil tinkling on the piano under a vast Landseer oil painting entitled 'The Swannery invaded by Sea Eagles' – a romantic scene of predatory eagles biting the heads off swans. Inspired by this example she pounced on her defenceless quarry and carried him off.

Christine was 'studying' at York University; Neil was several light years away at Aberystwyth. They carried on a long distance courtship by means of brief encounters – though not, like the film, on railway stations. After graduation, Neil decided to stay on as a research student. Christine decided she was not quite ready to enter the real world either so she found a job at the House of Commons working for the magniloquent and memorably moustachioed Sir Gerald Nabarro MP, whom she had met when he visited York University and who did not seem to mind her almost complete lack of secretarial skills. He was only interested in her mind.

While Neil was eking out an existence in circumstances resembling the set of *La Bohème*, living on a pittance, Christine was being courted a-plenty and taken out to lunch and dinner at ritzy establishments like . . . well, the Ritz (London, that is, not Paris!). The joys of conducting a romance with a student boyfriend who lived on the shores of Cardigan Bay, then a day's journey from London, quickly palled. Neil did not offer enough excitement (although he has made up for it since) and he had to go.

Unknown to him, Christine determined to perform her impression of Lady Macbeth and despatch him into amatory history. They were due to attend a Conservative Students conference together at Lancaster University, including a dinner to be addressed by the then Prime Minister, Edward Heath, at the unforgettably-named Dixieland Palace at Morecambe. Amongst the potted plants in the Palm Court the young Battleaxe struck. The evil deed was done.

Neil retraced his steps miserably back from Morecambe, on the sea-shore road down which he had driven earlier in the evening. Careering wildly along the deserted road, he suddenly hit what appeared to be a wall of water. He had failed to notice earlier that this road was a causeway. It had been low tide then. But now it was high tide and he had driven into four feet of seawater. He tried to present this as a romantic attempt to commit suicide by throwing himself into the sea. But Christine was not impressed by failure!

After several years of separation, Christine recognised her error of judgment and they spliced themselves together again. In spite of all setbacks, including the loss of Neil's seat and both their incomes (Christine worked full-time for him in the House of Commons) she has bounced back to cope with an almost impossible situation. She said 'I would fight the world on Neil's behalf. We have set about rebuilding our lives. We have done it before. We can do it again. We've hit a rock but we will go on.'

Christine originally thought of becoming an MP herself, but quickly thought again on seeing some of the nasty side of politics – the backstabbing and backbiting. Her recent problems at the eye of the storm now make that decision seem rather ironic.

For the last thirty years they have both devoted themselves to politics, only to see their careers destroyed on 1 May 1997. Suddenly losing such an all-consuming vocation can produce feelings of deprivation akin to bereavement. Sensing this, Robert Hardman of the *Daily Telegraph* had the temerity to ask Christine if she had considered counselling. He described the response: 'I might as well have asked about a past flirtation with CND. "Counselling?" she replies in pure Lady Bracknell. "Tosh!"'

Three years of nail-biting legal actions and Parliamentary Inquiries, the intrusions of the media ratpack with their telephoto lenses, the appalling one-sided publicity, the loss of job and income . . . a battering like this might destroy a lesser woman. Where does she get her indomitability from? Like Pitt the Younger she is 'not just a chip off the old block, but the old block itself.' The reaction of Neil's formidable mother-in-law, when Christine temporarily weakened one day, was to tell her to shape up and pull herself together, 'My dear, we went through the war. This is nothing!'

In fact, as Christine said to one interviewer, 'I'm not the wife from Hell. I'm as soft and vulnerable as anyone else. I make no secret of the fact I've been right down to the floor in floods of tears and feeling my body literally shaking with frustration, anger and unfairness. There have been moments when I've looked in the mirror and I've seen it all there. Etched.'

When a journalist reminded her of the 'laser-beam eyes' at the Battle of Knutsford Heath that so damaged her image, she shook her head in disbelief. 'I was horrified when I saw on television how aggressive I appeared . . . It might sound strange to an outsider but I'm not an aggressive personality. Yes, my appearance of strength did damage Neil but it happened really before we realised it. We didn't immediately see the danger of my appearing so formidable.

After all, it was just silly old me.'

But that was not the perception. Porky Alan Rusbridger (Christine thinks 'Rubbishwriter' would be more apt), Editor of the *Guardian* cowered in the *Newsnight* studio in October 1996 after a particularly bruising encounter with Neil, having been told by BBC staff that, 'Christine Hamilton is offering to plant one on your nose. We suggest you leave by another exit.' He refused to leave the sanctum of the studio until he knew she was safely out of the building.

He needn't have worried. She's never hit anyone in her life and, in any event, wouldn't have soiled her hands. Besides, but for his newspaper she would never have become a Battleaxe – and this book would never have been written.